Mozza Magic: A Culinary Journey with 100 Inspired Creations from Nancy Silverton's Iconic Restaurant

Hearty Slow Cooked Corn

:

Contents

INTRODUCTION

"Mozza Magic: A Culinary Journey with 100 Inspired Creations from Nancy Silverton's Iconic Restaurant"

Welcome to the culinary wonderland that is "Mozza Magic," a cookbook that invites you on an enchanting journey through the flavors, techniques, and inspirations that define the renowned Mozza restaurant, curated by the culinary maestro, Nancy Silverton. In the pages that follow, you will discover a treasure trove of 100 inspired creations, each a testament to the magic that unfolds in the heart of Mozza's kitchen.

Nancy Silverton, a trailblazing force in the culinary world, has not only mastered the art of crafting exceptional dishes but has also transformed the way we experience food. With Mozza, her iconic restaurant, she has redefined the dining landscape, elevating it to an extraordinary realm where flavors dance, textures sing, and every bite tells a story. "Mozza Magic" is a celebration of this culinary brilliance, a collection of recipes that pays homage to the soul of Mozza and the creativity that flows from its kitchen.

At the heart of this cookbook lies a curated selection of 100 food ideas, each meticulously crafted to reflect the essence of Mozza's menu. Whether you're a seasoned chef or a home cook eager to explore new horizons, these recipes offer a glimpse into the gastronomic wonders that have made Mozza a beacon in the culinary world.

The dishes within "Mozza Magic" are not merely recipes; they are a sensory experience. From the first page to the last, you'll embark on a culinary adventure that spans appetizers to desserts, showcasing the diversity and depth of Mozza's menu. Imagine recreating the legendary Mozza Caprese, where the simplicity of fresh mozzarella, tomatoes, and basil converges to create a symphony of flavors. Picture yourself mastering the art of handmade pasta with Mozza's signature Orecchiette with Sausage and Swiss Chard, or indulging in the decadence of the Butterscotch Budino that has become synonymous with dessert perfection at Mozza.

But "Mozza Magic" is more than a collection of recipes; it's a journey into the philosophy that defines Nancy Silverton's approach to food. Each dish is a manifestation of her commitment to using the finest ingredients, marrying tradition with innovation, and honoring the communal spirit of dining. Through the pages of this cookbook, you'll not only learn the techniques behind Mozza's culinary masterpieces but also gain insight into the stories, inspirations, and anecdotes that shape the restaurant's rich tapestry.

As you navigate through the chapters, you'll find yourself immersed in the world of Mozza – a world where culinary excellence meets unbridled creativity. Whether you're looking to recreate the magic of Mozza in your own kitchen or simply savor the journey through its iconic dishes, this cookbook is your passport to a culinary adventure like no other.

So, buckle up and get ready to embark on a gastronomic odyssey with "Mozza Magic." Let the pages inspire you, the recipes guide you, and the spirit of Mozza enchant you as you bring the magic of Nancy Silverton's iconic restaurant into your own home.

1. Burrata with Bacon, Escarole, and Caramelized Shallots

Indulge in the rich flavors and sophisticated combinations inspired by the renowned menu of Nancy Silverton's Mozza restaurant. This Burrata with Bacon, Escarole, and Caramelized Shallots dish brings together creamy burrata cheese, smoky bacon, crisp escarole, and the sweet essence of caramelized shallots. Elevate your dining experience with this tantalizing creation that embodies the culinary excellence of Mozza.

Serving: 4 servings
Preparation Time: 15 minutes
Ready Time: 30 minutes

Ingredients:
- 4 pieces of Burrata cheese
- 8 slices of bacon, cooked until crispy and crumbled
- 1 large head of escarole, washed and torn into bite-sized pieces
- 4 shallots, thinly sliced
- 2 tablespoons olive oil
- Salt and pepper to taste

Instructions:
1. Caramelize the Shallots:
- In a skillet over medium heat, add olive oil.
- Add thinly sliced shallots and sauté until golden brown and caramelized. This may take about 10-15 minutes. Set aside.
2. Prepare the Bacon:
- Cook bacon until it's crispy. Once done, crumble it into bite-sized pieces. Set aside.
3. Prepare the Escarole:
- Wash the escarole thoroughly and tear it into bite-sized pieces.
4. Assemble the Dish:
- On each serving plate, place a piece of Burrata cheese in the center.
- Surround the Burrata with the torn escarole leaves.
- Sprinkle the crispy bacon crumbles over the escarole.
- Top the dish with a generous portion of caramelized shallots.
5. Season and Serve:

- Drizzle olive oil over the burrata and escarole.
- Season with salt and pepper to taste.

Nutrition Information:
- *Note: Nutritional values are approximate and may vary based on specific ingredients used.*
- Calories: XXX per serving
- Fat: XXXg
- Saturated Fat: XXXg
- Cholesterol: XXXmg
- Sodium: XXXmg
- Carbohydrates: XXXg
- Fiber: XXXg
- Sugars: XXXg
- Protein: XXXg

Enjoy the delightful harmony of flavors in this Burrata with Bacon, Escarole, and Caramelized Shallots dish – a tribute to the culinary brilliance of Nancy Silverton's Mozza restaurant.

2. Grilled Octopus with Lemon, Potatoes, and Celery

Step into the culinary world inspired by the renowned Nancy Silverton's Mozza restaurant with this exquisite recipe for Grilled Octopus with Lemon, Potatoes, and Celery. Immerse yourself in the rich flavors and textures of this dish, which captures the essence of Mozza's commitment to quality ingredients and expert craftsmanship. The combination of tender grilled octopus, zesty lemon, creamy potatoes, and crisp celery creates a symphony of tastes that will elevate your dining experience.

Serving: ---
This recipe serves 4.
Preparation Time: ---
- 20 minutes

Ready Time: ---
- 1 hour and 30 minutes

Ingredients:

- 2 pounds octopus, cleaned and tentacles separated
- 1/4 cup olive oil
- 2 cloves garlic, minced
- 1 teaspoon smoked paprika
- Salt and black pepper to taste
- 4 medium-sized potatoes, peeled and diced
- 1 cup celery, thinly sliced
- Zest of 1 lemon
- Juice of 2 lemons
- 2 tablespoons fresh parsley, chopped

Instructions:

---

1. Preheat your grill to medium-high heat.
2. In a bowl, combine olive oil, minced garlic, smoked paprika, salt, and black pepper. Add the cleaned octopus tentacles, ensuring they are well-coated with the marinade. Allow it to marinate for 30 minutes.
3. While the octopus is marinating, boil the diced potatoes until they are fork-tender. Drain and set aside.
4. Grill the marinated octopus for about 4-5 minutes per side or until it develops a nice char and is cooked through. Remove from the grill and let it rest for a few minutes.
5. In a large bowl, combine the grilled octopus, boiled potatoes, sliced celery, lemon zest, lemon juice, and chopped parsley. Toss gently to combine all the flavors.
6. Serve the Grilled Octopus with Lemon, Potatoes, and Celery on a platter, garnished with extra parsley and lemon wedges.

Nutrition Information:

Note: Nutrition information is approximate and may vary based on specific ingredients used.
- Calories per serving: 350
- Total Fat: 15g
- Saturated Fat: 2.5g
- Trans Fat: 0g
- Cholesterol: 50mg
- Sodium: 300mg
- Total Carbohydrates: 35g

- Dietary Fiber: 5g
- Sugars: 3g
- Protein: 20g

Indulge in the culinary magic inspired by Nancy Silverton's Mozza with this Grilled Octopus recipe, a true celebration of flavors and textures.

3. Margherita Pizza with Tomato, Fresh Mozzarella, and Basil

Indulge in the classic simplicity of a Margherita Pizza inspired by the culinary brilliance of Nancy Silverton's Mozza restaurant. This timeless dish celebrates the trinity of flavors with ripe tomatoes, creamy fresh mozzarella, and fragrant basil, all on a perfectly crisp crust. The Mozza touch elevates this pizza to a culinary masterpiece that pays homage to the authentic Italian tradition.

Serving: Makes one 12-inch pizza, serving 2-4 people.
Preparation Time: 15 minutes
Ready Time: 20 minutes

Ingredients:
- 1 pizza dough ball (store-bought or homemade)
- 1/2 cup pizza sauce
- 2 medium-sized ripe tomatoes, thinly sliced
- 8 ounces fresh mozzarella, sliced
- Fresh basil leaves, for garnish
- Extra-virgin olive oil, for drizzling
- Salt and pepper to taste

Instructions:
1. Preheat the Oven:
Preheat your oven to the highest temperature it can reach (usually around 475-500°F or 245-260°C). If you have a pizza stone, place it in the oven while preheating.
2. Prepare the Dough:
Roll out the pizza dough on a floured surface to your desired thickness. If you have a pizza peel, transfer the rolled-out dough onto it.
3. Assemble the Pizza:

Spread a thin layer of pizza sauce evenly over the dough, leaving a small border for the crust. Arrange the sliced tomatoes and fresh mozzarella on top. Season with salt and pepper.
4. Bake the Pizza:
If you have a pizza stone, carefully transfer the pizza onto the hot stone in the oven. If not, place the pizza on a baking sheet. Bake for 12-15 minutes or until the crust is golden and the cheese is melted and bubbly.
5. Finish with Fresh Basil and Olive Oil:
Once out of the oven, scatter fresh basil leaves over the hot pizza. Drizzle with extra-virgin olive oil for added richness and flavor.
6. Slice and Serve:
Allow the pizza to cool for a couple of minutes before slicing. Serve hot and savor the delectable combination of flavors.

Nutrition Information:
(Per Serving - Assumes 4 servings)
- Calories: 350
- Total Fat: 12g
- Saturated Fat: 6g
- Cholesterol: 30mg
- Sodium: 650mg
- Total Carbohydrates: 45g
- Dietary Fiber: 2g
- Sugars: 4g
- Protein: 15g

Note: Nutrition information is approximate and may vary based on specific ingredients and portion sizes.

4. Squash Blossom Pizza with Tomato, Zucchini, and Burrata

Indulge in the culinary magic inspired by the renowned Mozza restaurant, where Nancy Silverton's expertise transforms every dish into a symphony of flavors. This Squash Blossom Pizza with Tomato, Zucchini, and Burrata is a celebration of fresh, seasonal ingredients, echoing the vibrant and innovative spirit of Mozza's menu.

Serving: 4 servings

Preparation Time: 20 minutes
Ready Time: 15 minutes

Ingredients:
- 1 pound pizza dough (store-bought or homemade)
- 1/2 cup tomato sauce
- 1 medium zucchini, thinly sliced
- 1 cup squash blossoms, cleaned and petals separated
- 1 ball Burrata cheese, torn into pieces
- 1/4 cup extra-virgin olive oil
- Salt and pepper to taste
- Cornmeal or flour for dusting (for rolling out the dough)

Instructions:
1. Preheat the Oven:
Preheat your oven to the highest temperature it can go, typically around 475°F (245°C).
2. Prepare the Dough:
If using store-bought dough, let it come to room temperature. On a lightly floured surface, roll out the dough to your desired thickness.
3. Assemble the Pizza:
Place the rolled-out dough on a pizza stone or a baking sheet dusted with cornmeal or flour. Spread an even layer of tomato sauce over the dough, leaving a small border around the edges.
4. Add the Toppings:
Arrange the zucchini slices evenly on the pizza. Sprinkle the squash blossom petals over the zucchini. Place torn pieces of Burrata on top. Drizzle with olive oil and season with salt and pepper.
5. Bake:
Transfer the pizza to the preheated oven and bake until the crust is golden and the toppings are bubbly and slightly browned, approximately 12-15 minutes.
6. Finish and Serve:
Remove the pizza from the oven, allowing it to cool for a few minutes. Slice and serve, embracing the melty goodness of Burrata and the delicate flavors of squash blossoms.

Nutrition Information:
Note: Nutrition information is approximate and may vary based on specific ingredients and portion sizes.

- Calories: 400 per serving
- Total Fat: 20g
- Saturated Fat: 7g
- Cholesterol: 30mg
- Sodium: 700mg
- Total Carbohydrates: 45g
- Dietary Fiber: 3g
- Sugars: 3g
- Protein: 12g

Embrace the culinary journey inspired by Nancy Silverton's Mozza restaurant with this Squash Blossom Pizza, where each bite tells a story of freshness, creativity, and the love for good food.

5. Prosciutto and Melon Salad with Mint and Pecorino

Indulge in the culinary symphony of flavors with our Prosciutto and Melon Salad inspired by the delectable offerings at Nancy Silverton's renowned Mozza restaurant. This refreshing and elegant dish perfectly balances the sweet essence of ripe melon with the savory allure of prosciutto, all elevated by the aromatic notes of fresh mint and the nutty richness of Pecorino. Elevate your dining experience with this exquisite salad that captures the essence of Mozza's sophisticated menu.

Serving: 4 servings
Preparation Time: 15 minutes
Ready Time: 15 minutes

Ingredients:
- 1 ripe cantaloupe, peeled, seeded, and cut into thin wedges
- 8 thin slices of prosciutto
- 1/2 cup Pecorino cheese, shaved
- Fresh mint leaves, for garnish

Dressing:
- 2 tablespoons extra-virgin olive oil
- 1 tablespoon balsamic vinegar
- Salt and pepper, to taste

Instructions:

1. Prepare the Dressing: In a small bowl, whisk together the olive oil, balsamic vinegar, salt, and pepper. Set aside.
2. Assemble the Salad: On a serving platter, arrange the cantaloupe wedges.
3. Layer with Prosciutto: Drape the thin slices of prosciutto over the cantaloupe, creating a harmonious blend of sweet and savory.
4. Add Pecorino Shavings: Scatter Pecorino shavings generously over the salad, ensuring a distribution of nutty richness.
5. Drizzle with Dressing: Drizzle the prepared dressing over the salad, allowing the flavors to mingle.
6. Garnish with Mint: Sprinkle fresh mint leaves on top for a burst of aromatic freshness.
7. Serve: Serve immediately, allowing your guests to experience the perfect harmony of textures and flavors.

Nutrition Information:

(Per serving)

- Calories: 180
- Total Fat: 10g
- Saturated Fat: 3g
- Trans Fat: 0g
- Cholesterol: 20mg
- Sodium: 600mg
- Total Carbohydrates: 15g
- Dietary Fiber: 2g
- Sugars: 11g
- Protein: 9g

Note: Nutrition information is approximate and may vary based on specific ingredients used. Adjustments can be made to suit dietary preferences or restrictions.

6. Mozzarella and Speck Panini with Basil Pesto

Indulge in the culinary wonders inspired by the famed Mozza restaurant, where Chef Nancy Silverton's artistry transforms everyday ingredients into extraordinary dishes. Among the delectable offerings is the Mozzarella and Speck Panini with Basil Pesto—a harmonious blend of rich mozzarella, savory speck, and vibrant basil pesto, encapsulated within the warmth of a perfectly grilled panini. Elevate your home cooking experience with this delightful recipe that captures the essence of Mozza's culinary brilliance.

Serving: Makes 2 paninis
Preparation Time: 15 minutes
Ready Time: 25 minutes

Ingredients:
- 4 slices of rustic Italian bread
- 8 ounces fresh mozzarella, sliced
- 6 slices of speck (smoked prosciutto)
- 1/2 cup fresh basil leaves
- 1/4 cup pine nuts, toasted
- 1/2 cup grated Parmesan cheese
- 2 garlic cloves, minced
- 1/2 cup extra-virgin olive oil
- Salt and pepper to taste
- Unsalted butter, for spreading on bread

Instructions:
1. Prepare the Basil Pesto:
a. In a food processor, combine the fresh basil, toasted pine nuts, Parmesan cheese, and minced garlic.
b. Pulse until ingredients are finely chopped.
c. With the processor running, slowly add the olive oil until the pesto reaches a smooth consistency.
d. Season with salt and pepper to taste. Set aside.
2. Assemble the Panini:
a. Lay out four slices of rustic Italian bread.
b. Spread a generous layer of the prepared basil pesto on each slice.
c. On two of the slices, layer the fresh mozzarella and speck evenly.
d. Top each with the remaining slices of bread, pesto side down, creating two sandwiches.
3. Grill the Panini:
a. Heat a panini press or grill pan over medium heat.
b. Spread a thin layer of unsalted butter on the outside of each sandwich.
c. Grill the paninis for 4-5 minutes, or until the bread is golden brown, and the mozzarella has melted.

4. Serve:
a. Carefully remove the paninis from the press or pan.
b. Allow them to cool for a minute before slicing.
c. Serve warm and enjoy the gooey mozzarella, savory speck, and aromatic basil pesto melding together in every bite.

Nutrition Information:
(Per Serving)
- Calories: 650
- Total Fat: 52g
- Saturated Fat: 16g
- Trans Fat: 0g
- Cholesterol: 70mg
- Sodium: 980mg
- Total Carbohydrates: 22g
- Dietary Fiber: 3g
- Sugars: 2g
- Protein: 23g

Note: Nutrition information is approximate and may vary based on specific ingredients used.

7. Ricotta and Egg Raviolo with Brown Butter and Sage

Indulge in the exquisite flavors of Nancy Silverton's Mozza restaurant with this delightful recipe for Ricotta and Egg Raviolo with Brown Butter and Sage. Inspired by the restaurant's commitment to quality and innovation, this dish is a perfect blend of rich ricotta, runny egg yolk, and the nutty warmth of brown butter and sage. Elevate your home cooking experience with this luxurious pasta creation that captures the essence of Mozza's culinary expertise.

Serving: 4 servings
Preparation Time: 30 minutes
Ready Time: 45 minutes

Ingredients:
- 2 cups fresh ricotta cheese

- 4 large eggs
- 1 cup freshly grated Parmesan cheese
- Salt and black pepper, to taste
- 1 package square wonton wrappers
- 1/2 cup unsalted butter
- Fresh sage leaves
- Extra Parmesan for garnish

Instructions:

1. Prepare the Filling:
In a mixing bowl, combine fresh ricotta, grated Parmesan, salt, and black pepper. Mix well until the ingredients are evenly incorporated.
2. Assemble the Ravioli:
Place a wonton wrapper on a clean surface. Spoon a generous dollop of the ricotta mixture onto the center of the wrapper. Create a well in the center and carefully crack an egg into it. Be cautious not to break the yolk. Repeat for the remaining wrappers.
3. Seal and Shape:
Moisten the edges of each wrapper with water and fold them into a triangle, sealing the edges to encase the egg and ricotta filling. Press firmly to remove any air bubbles. Ensure a tight seal to prevent the egg from leaking during cooking.
4. Cook the Ravioli:
Bring a large pot of salted water to a gentle simmer. Carefully add the ravioli and cook for about 3-4 minutes or until the pasta is tender and the egg yolk is still runny.
5. Prepare the Brown Butter and Sage Sauce:
In a separate pan, melt the butter over medium heat. Add fresh sage leaves and cook until the butter turns a rich golden brown, and the sage becomes crispy. Remove from heat.
6. Serve:
Gently transfer the cooked ravioli onto plates. Drizzle the brown butter and sage sauce over the top. Garnish with extra Parmesan and freshly ground black pepper.

Nutrition Information:

(Per serving)
- Calories: XXX
- Protein: XXXg
- Carbohydrates: XXXg

- Fat: XXXg
- Fiber: XXXg
- Sugar: XXXg
- Sodium: XXXmg

Indulge in the luscious combination of creamy ricotta, velvety egg yolk, and the aromatic notes of brown butter and sage. This Ricotta and Egg Raviolo pays homage to the culinary excellence of Nancy Silverton's Mozza, bringing a touch of sophistication to your home kitchen.

8. Grilled Branzino with Salsa Verde and Charred Lemon

Indulge in the exquisite flavors of Nancy Silverton's Mozza restaurant with this Grilled Branzino with Salsa Verde and Charred Lemon recipe. A dish that encapsulates the essence of the renowned establishment, it combines the delicate tenderness of branzino with the vibrant zing of salsa verde, all elevated by the smoky notes of charred lemon. Immerse yourself in the culinary artistry inspired by Mozza, bringing a touch of sophistication to your own kitchen.

Serving: Serves 4
Preparation Time: 20 minutes
Ready Time: 30 minutes

Ingredients:
- 2 whole branzino, cleaned and scaled
- Salt and black pepper, to taste
- 2 lemons, halved
- Olive oil, for brushing

For Salsa Verde:
- 1 cup fresh parsley, finely chopped
- 1/2 cup fresh basil, finely chopped
- 2 tablespoons capers, drained and chopped
- 2 cloves garlic, minced
- 1 tablespoon Dijon mustard
- 1 tablespoon red wine vinegar
- 1/2 cup extra-virgin olive oil
- Salt and black pepper, to taste

Instructions:

1. Prepare the Salsa Verde:
- In a bowl, combine the chopped parsley, basil, capers, minced garlic, Dijon mustard, and red wine vinegar.
- Gradually whisk in the extra-virgin olive oil until the salsa verde is well blended.
- Season with salt and black pepper to taste. Set aside.
2. Prepare the Branzino:
- Preheat the grill to medium-high heat.
- Score the skin of the branzino with diagonal cuts on both sides.
- Season the fish generously with salt and black pepper, inside and out.
- Brush the branzino with olive oil.
3. Grill the Branzino:
- Place the branzino on the preheated grill and cook for about 4-5 minutes per side, or until the skin is crispy and the flesh is opaque and flakes easily.
- During the last few minutes of grilling, add the lemon halves to the grill, cut side down, until they are charred and caramelized.
4. Serve:
- Transfer the grilled branzino to a serving platter.
- Spoon the salsa verde generously over the fish.
- Squeeze the charred lemon over the branzino before serving.

Nutrition Information:

(Per serving)
- Calories: 350
- Protein: 28g
- Fat: 20g
- Carbohydrates: 10g
- Fiber: 3g

Indulge in the symphony of flavors as you savor this Grilled Branzino with Salsa Verde and Charred Lemon, inspired by the culinary wonders of Nancy Silverton's Mozza restaurant.

9. Roasted Beet and Goat Cheese Salad with Pistachios

Indulge in the vibrant flavors and exquisite textures inspired by the culinary mastery of Nancy Silverton's Mozza restaurant with this Roasted Beet and Goat Cheese Salad with Pistachios. This salad is a symphony of earthy roasted beets, creamy goat cheese, and crunchy pistachios, creating a delightful harmony on your plate. Elevate your dining experience with this simple yet sophisticated dish that captures the essence of Mozza's renowned menu.

Serving: 4 servings
Preparation time: 15 minutes
Ready time: 1 hour (including roasting time)

Ingredients:
- 4 medium-sized beets, peeled and diced
- 2 tablespoons olive oil
- Salt and pepper, to taste
- 4 cups mixed salad greens (arugula, spinach, and/or watercress)
- 1/2 cup goat cheese, crumbled
- 1/2 cup pistachios, toasted and chopped

Instructions:
1. Preheat the oven: Preheat your oven to 400°F (200°C).
2. Roast the beets: Place the diced beets on a baking sheet. Drizzle with olive oil, and season with salt and pepper. Toss to coat evenly. Roast in the preheated oven for about 40-45 minutes or until the beets are tender and slightly caramelized. Allow them to cool.
3. Prepare the salad greens: In a large bowl, combine the mixed salad greens.
4. Assemble the salad: Add the roasted beets to the salad greens. Sprinkle crumbled goat cheese and toasted, chopped pistachios over the top.
5. Toss gently: Toss the salad gently to combine all the ingredients evenly.
6. Serve: Divide the salad among four plates, ensuring a colorful and balanced distribution of beets, goat cheese, and pistachios.
7. Enjoy: Delight in the contrasting textures and flavors of the roasted beets, creamy goat cheese, and crunchy pistachios.

Nutrition Information:
(Per serving)
- Calories: 250

- Total Fat: 18g
- Saturated Fat: 6g
- Trans Fat: 0g
- Cholesterol: 15mg
- Sodium: 220mg
- Total Carbohydrates: 18g
- Dietary Fiber: 4g
- Sugars: 10g
- Protein: 8g

Note: Nutrition Information is approximate and may vary based on specific ingredients and portion sizes.

10. Fennel Sausage Pizza with Tomato and Mozzarella

Indulge your taste buds in the culinary magic inspired by Nancy Silverton's iconic Mozza restaurant with our Fennel Sausage Pizza. This delectable creation combines the bold flavors of fennel-infused sausage, ripe tomatoes, and creamy mozzarella, paying homage to the irresistible charm of Mozza's menu. Elevate your pizza experience with this savory delight that captures the essence of Silverton's culinary expertise.

Serving: Makes 1 large pizza (approximately 8 slices)
Preparation Time: 15 minutes
Ready Time: 30 minutes

Ingredients:

- 1 pizza dough (store-bought or homemade)
- 1/2 cup pizza sauce
- 1 cup shredded mozzarella cheese
- 1/2 cup sliced cherry tomatoes
- 1/2 pound fennel sausage, cooked and crumbled
- 1/4 cup grated Parmesan cheese
- 1 tablespoon olive oil
- 1 teaspoon dried oregano
- Salt and pepper to taste
- Fresh basil leaves for garnish (optional)

Instructions:
1. Preheat your oven to 475°F (245°C). If you have a pizza stone, place it in the oven to heat.
2. Roll out the pizza dough on a floured surface to your desired thickness. If using a pizza stone, transfer the rolled-out dough to a pizza peel or another flat, floured surface.
3. Spread the pizza sauce evenly over the dough, leaving a small border around the edges for the crust.
4. Sprinkle the shredded mozzarella cheese over the sauce, followed by the sliced cherry tomatoes and crumbled fennel sausage.
5. Drizzle olive oil over the pizza and sprinkle with grated Parmesan cheese. Season with dried oregano, salt, and pepper to taste.
6. If using a pizza stone, carefully transfer the pizza to the preheated stone in the oven. If not using a stone, place the pizza on a baking sheet.
7. Bake for 12-15 minutes or until the crust is golden and the cheese is melted and bubbly.
8. Remove the pizza from the oven and let it cool for a few minutes before slicing. Garnish with fresh basil leaves if desired.

Nutrition Information:
(Per slice, based on 8 slices)
- Calories: approximately 250
- Total Fat: 12g
- Saturated Fat: 5g
- Cholesterol: 25mg
- Sodium: 600mg
- Total Carbohydrates: 24g
- Dietary Fiber: 1g
- Sugars: 2g
- Protein: 12g

Note: Nutrition information is approximate and may vary based on specific ingredients and portion sizes. Adjustments can be made for dietary preferences and restrictions.

11. Marinated White Anchovies with Celery and Lemon

Indulge in the culinary delights inspired by the iconic Mozza restaurant with this exquisite recipe for Marinated White Anchovies with Celery and Lemon. The dish captures the essence of Nancy Silverton's renowned establishment, where bold flavors and exceptional ingredients come together in perfect harmony. Elevate your dining experience with these delectable marinated white anchovies, complemented by the crisp freshness of celery and the zesty kick of lemon.

Serving: 4 servings
Preparation Time: 15 minutes
Ready Time: 2 hours (including marination time)

Ingredients:
- 1 pound fresh white anchovy fillets
- 4 celery stalks, thinly sliced
- Zest of 1 lemon
- 1/4 cup fresh lemon juice
- 1/3 cup extra-virgin olive oil
- 2 cloves garlic, minced
- 1 tablespoon fresh parsley, finely chopped
- Salt and black pepper to taste

Instructions:
1. Prepare the Anchovies:
- Rinse the white anchovy fillets under cold water and pat them dry with paper towels.
- Carefully remove any bones or scales from the fillets.
2. Marinate the Anchovies:
- In a bowl, whisk together the lemon zest, lemon juice, olive oil, minced garlic, chopped parsley, salt, and black pepper.
- Place the anchovy fillets in a shallow dish and pour the marinade over them, ensuring each fillet is well coated.
- Cover the dish and refrigerate for at least 2 hours to allow the flavors to meld.
3. Prepare the Celery:
- While the anchovies are marinating, thinly slice the celery stalks. If desired, you can use a mandoline for uniform slices.
4. Assemble the Dish:
- Arrange the marinated white anchovies on a serving platter.

- Scatter the sliced celery over the anchovies, creating a visually appealing and flavorful combination.
5. Final Touch:
- Drizzle any remaining marinade over the top for an extra burst of flavor.
- Garnish with additional chopped parsley for a fresh and vibrant finish.
6. Serve:
- Serve the Marinated White Anchovies with Celery and Lemon as an appetizer or part of a tapas spread. Pair with crusty bread or crackers to enjoy the full spectrum of flavors.

Nutrition Information:
Note: Nutritional values are approximate and may vary based on specific ingredients used.
- Calories: 180 per serving
- Protein: 15g
- Fat: 12g
- Carbohydrates: 4g
- Fiber: 1g
- Sugar: 1g
- Sodium: 420mg

Indulge in this culinary masterpiece inspired by Nancy Silverton's Mozza restaurant, where each bite tells a story of innovation and unparalleled taste.

12. Wood-Grilled Lamb Chops with Rosemary and Garlic

Indulge in the robust flavors of Nancy Silverton's Mozza restaurant with these Wood-Grilled Lamb Chops with Rosemary and Garlic. Inspired by the culinary excellence of Mozza, this dish combines the earthy essence of wood-grilled lamb with aromatic rosemary and the rich undertones of garlic. Elevate your dining experience with this delectable recipe that captures the essence of Mozza's renowned menu.

Serving: 4 servings
Preparation Time: 15 minutes
Ready Time: 1 hour and 15 minutes (including marination and grilling)

Ingredients:

- 8 lamb chops, about 1 inch thick
- 4 cloves garlic, minced
- 2 tablespoons fresh rosemary, finely chopped
- 1/4 cup olive oil
- Salt and black pepper to taste
- Lemon wedges for garnish

Instructions:

1. Marinate the Lamb Chops:
- In a bowl, combine minced garlic, chopped rosemary, olive oil, salt, and black pepper.
- Place lamb chops in a large dish and generously coat them with the marinade, ensuring each chop is well covered.
- Cover the dish and let the lamb marinate in the refrigerator for at least 1 hour, allowing the flavors to infuse.

2. Preheat the Grill:
- Prepare a wood-fired grill for medium-high heat. The wood smoke adds a unique flavor to the lamb.

3. Grill the Lamb Chops:
- Remove the lamb chops from the marinade and let any excess drip off.
- Place the chops on the preheated grill and cook for about 5-7 minutes per side, or until the internal temperature reaches your desired doneness.
- For medium-rare, aim for an internal temperature of 145°F (63°C).

4. Rest and Serve:
- Allow the grilled lamb chops to rest for a few minutes before serving. This helps the juices redistribute, ensuring a moist and flavorful bite.
- Serve the wood-grilled lamb chops with lemon wedges for a burst of citrus freshness.

Nutrition Information:

Note: Nutrition information is approximate and may vary based on specific ingredients and cooking methods.

- Calories per serving: 380
- Protein: 32g
- Fat: 25g
- Carbohydrates: 2g
- Fiber: 1g

Savor the essence of Mozza's culinary artistry with these Wood-Grilled Lamb Chops— a dish that perfectly encapsulates the bold and sophisticated flavors that define the renowned restaurant's menu.

13. Tomato and Stracciatella Bruschetta with Basil

Indulge your taste buds in the vibrant flavors of Nancy Silverton's Mozza restaurant with this exquisite Tomato and Stracciatella Bruschetta with Basil. A delightful blend of fresh tomatoes, creamy stracciatella cheese, and fragrant basil, this bruschetta embodies the essence of Italian cuisine. It's a celebration of simple yet sophisticated ingredients that come together to create a burst of Mediterranean goodness on your plate.

Serving: Serves 4
Preparation Time: 15 minutes
Ready Time: 20 minutes

Ingredients:
- 4 large ripe tomatoes, diced
- 8 ounces stracciatella cheese
- 1/4 cup fresh basil leaves, thinly sliced
- 2 cloves garlic, minced
- 3 tablespoons extra-virgin olive oil
- Salt and pepper to taste
- 1 French baguette, sliced diagonally into 1/2-inch thick pieces

Instructions:
1. In a large bowl, combine the diced tomatoes, minced garlic, and sliced basil. Drizzle with 2 tablespoons of olive oil and gently toss to coat. Season with salt and pepper to taste. Set aside to let the flavors meld.
2. Preheat the oven to 375°F (190°C).
3. Arrange the baguette slices on a baking sheet and brush each slice with the remaining tablespoon of olive oil. Toast in the preheated oven for 5-7 minutes or until the edges are golden brown.
4. While the bread is toasting, assemble the bruschetta. Spread a generous portion of stracciatella cheese on each toasted baguette slice.
5. Top the cheese with the tomato and basil mixture, ensuring an even distribution of flavors on each bruschetta.

6. Serve immediately, allowing your guests to experience the delightful combination of textures and tastes.

Nutrition Information:
(Per serving)
- Calories: 320
- Total Fat: 20g
- Saturated Fat: 8g
- Cholesterol: 30mg
- Sodium: 480mg
- Total Carbohydrates: 25g
- Dietary Fiber: 3g
- Sugars: 4g
- Protein: 10g

Note: Nutrition information is approximate and may vary based on specific ingredients used. Adjust quantities according to dietary preferences and restrictions. Enjoy the Mozza-inspired goodness!

14. Grilled Asparagus with Prosciutto and Fried Egg

Inspired by the culinary brilliance of Nancy Silverton's Mozza restaurant, this recipe combines the earthy flavor of grilled asparagus with the rich, savory notes of prosciutto and a luscious fried egg. A perfect symphony of textures and tastes, this dish exemplifies the artistry of Mozza's menu. Whether enjoyed as a delightful appetizer or a satisfying brunch option, this Grilled Asparagus with Prosciutto and Fried Egg is sure to elevate your dining experience.

Serving: 4 servings
Preparation Time: 15 minutes
Ready Time: 25 minutes

Ingredients:
- 1 bunch of fresh asparagus, woody ends trimmed
- 8 slices of prosciutto
- 4 large eggs
- Olive oil for drizzling
- Salt and black pepper to taste

- Optional: Grated Parmesan cheese for garnish

Instructions:
1. Prepare the Grill:
Preheat your grill to medium-high heat. If using an indoor grill pan, make sure it's well-heated.
2. Grill the Asparagus:
Place the trimmed asparagus on the grill and drizzle with olive oil. Season with salt and pepper. Grill for 5-7 minutes, turning occasionally, until the asparagus is tender and has a slight char.
3. Wrap with Prosciutto:
While the asparagus is grilling, wrap each spear with a slice of prosciutto. The heat from the asparagus will slightly cook and crisp the prosciutto.
4. Fry the Eggs:
In a separate non-stick pan, fry the eggs to your desired doneness. For a runny yolk, this usually takes about 3-4 minutes.
5. Assemble:
Place the grilled asparagus bundles on a serving platter. Top each bundle with a fried egg. Drizzle with a bit more olive oil and season with additional salt and pepper if needed. Optionally, sprinkle grated Parmesan cheese over the top.
6. Serve:
Serve immediately, allowing the runny yolk to meld with the asparagus, creating a luxurious sauce.

Nutrition Information:
Note: Nutrition information is approximate and may vary based on specific ingredients used.
- Calories: 250 per serving
- Protein: 15g
- Fat: 18g
- Carbohydrates: 8g
- Fiber: 4g
- Sugar: 2g
Enjoy the delectable flavors of Mozza's inspiration in the comfort of your own home with this Grilled Asparagus with Prosciutto and Fried Egg.

15. Margherita Pizza with Prosciutto di Parma

Indulge in the culinary charm of Nancy Silverton's Mozza restaurant with our delightful Margherita Pizza topped with the exquisite Prosciutto di Parma. This recipe pays homage to the iconic flavors and meticulous craftsmanship synonymous with Mozza's menu. Revel in the perfect blend of fresh, high-quality ingredients that define the essence of Mozza's culinary legacy.

Serving: 4 servings
Preparation Time: 20 minutes
Ready Time: 15 minutes

Ingredients:
- 1 pound pizza dough (store-bought or homemade)
- 1/2 cup pizza sauce
- 8 ounces fresh mozzarella, sliced
- 1/4 cup fresh basil leaves, torn
- 4 slices Prosciutto di Parma
- 2 tablespoons extra-virgin olive oil
- Salt and pepper to taste

Instructions:
1. Preheat the Oven:
Preheat your oven to 475°F (245°C). If you have a pizza stone, place it in the oven during preheating.
2. Roll Out the Dough:
On a lightly floured surface, roll out the pizza dough to your desired thickness.
3. Prepare the Pizza:
a. If using a pizza stone, transfer the rolled-out dough onto a piece of parchment paper dusted with flour or cornmeal.
b. Spread the pizza sauce evenly over the dough, leaving a small border around the edges.
c. Arrange the fresh mozzarella slices on top of the sauce.
d. Add torn basil leaves and season with salt and pepper.
4. Bake the Pizza:
a. If using a pizza stone, carefully transfer the parchment paper with the pizza onto the hot stone in the oven.

b. Bake for 12-15 minutes or until the crust is golden and the cheese is bubbly and slightly browned.
5. Add Prosciutto di Parma:
a. Remove the pizza from the oven and drape the Prosciutto di Parma slices over the hot, melted cheese.
b. Drizzle the pizza with extra-virgin olive oil.
6. Slice and Serve:
Allow the pizza to cool for a few minutes before slicing. Serve hot and enjoy the luxurious blend of flavors.

Nutrition Information:
Note: Nutrition information is approximate and may vary based on specific ingredients and portion sizes.
- Calories: 450 per serving
- Total Fat: 22g
- Saturated Fat: 8g
- Trans Fat: 0g
- Cholesterol: 40mg
- Sodium: 900mg
- Total Carbohydrates: 45g
- Dietary Fiber: 2g
- Sugars: 2g
- Protein: 18g

Elevate your pizza experience with the Margherita Pizza with Prosciutto di Parma—a culinary masterpiece inspired by the renowned flavors of Nancy Silverton's Mozza restaurant.

16. Burrata with Cherry Tomatoes and Basil Pesto

Indulge your senses with the exquisite flavors inspired by the renowned Mozza restaurant, as we bring you a delectable dish featuring the finest ingredients - Burrata with Cherry Tomatoes and Basil Pesto. This dish perfectly captures the essence of Nancy Silverton's culinary artistry, combining the creaminess of burrata with the sweetness of ripe cherry tomatoes and the vibrant freshness of basil pesto. Elevate your dining experience with this easy-to-prepare, yet elegant recipe that embodies the essence of Mozza's menu.

Serving: 4 servings
Preparation Time: 15 minutes
Ready Time: 15 minutes

Ingredients:
- 4 large balls of burrata cheese
- 2 cups cherry tomatoes, halved
- 1/2 cup fresh basil leaves, thinly sliced
- 1/4 cup extra-virgin olive oil
- Salt and black pepper to taste
- 1/4 cup balsamic glaze (optional, for drizzling)

Instructions:
1. Prepare the Burrata:
- Carefully slice each ball of burrata in half, allowing the creamy interior to be exposed.
2. Arrange the Tomatoes:
- Place the halved cherry tomatoes around the burrata on a serving platter, creating a visually appealing arrangement.
3. Sprinkle with Basil:
- Generously sprinkle the sliced fresh basil leaves over the burrata and tomatoes, evenly distributing them for a burst of flavor in every bite.
4. Drizzle with Olive Oil:
- Drizzle extra-virgin olive oil over the entire dish, enhancing the creaminess of the burrata and adding a rich, fruity note.
5. Season to Perfection:
- Season the dish with salt and black pepper to taste, ensuring a harmonious balance of flavors.
6. Optional Drizzle:
- For an extra touch of sweetness, drizzle balsamic glaze over the burrata and tomatoes. This step is optional but highly recommended for a delightful contrast.
7. Serve Immediately:
- Burrata is at its best when served immediately after preparation. Allow your guests to experience the dish while the flavors are at their peak.

Nutrition Information:
(Per serving)
- Calories: 300
- Total Fat: 24g

- Saturated Fat: 10g
- Trans Fat: 0g
- Cholesterol: 50mg
- Sodium: 300mg
- Total Carbohydrates: 8g
- Dietary Fiber: 2g
- Sugars: 4g
- Protein: 15g

Indulge in the divine combination of creamy burrata, sweet cherry tomatoes, and aromatic basil pesto—a culinary masterpiece inspired by the iconic Mozza restaurant. This dish is a celebration of simplicity and quality ingredients, inviting you to savor the essence of Nancy Silverton's culinary expertise in the comfort of your own home.

17. Wood-Grilled Quail with Porcini and Polenta

Indulge in the rustic elegance of Nancy Silverton's Mozza restaurant with this exquisite Wood-Grilled Quail with Porcini and Polenta recipe. Inspired by the culinary artistry of Mozza, this dish seamlessly combines the earthy flavors of wood-grilled quail, the rich umami of porcini mushrooms, and the creamy perfection of polenta. Elevate your dining experience with a taste of Mozza's sophisticated charm right in the comfort of your own home.

Serving: This recipe serves 4.
Preparation Time: 30 minutes
Ready Time: 1 hour and 30 minutes

Ingredients:
- 4 quails, cleaned and butterflied
- 1 cup dried porcini mushrooms
- 2 cups boiling water
- 2 tablespoons olive oil
- 4 cloves garlic, minced
- 1 teaspoon fresh thyme leaves
- Salt and black pepper, to taste

For the Polenta:
- 1 cup polenta

- 4 cups chicken or vegetable broth
- 1 cup whole milk
- 1/2 cup grated Parmesan cheese
- Salt and black pepper, to taste

Instructions:
1. Rehydrate Porcini:
- Place dried porcini mushrooms in a bowl and pour boiling water over them. Let them soak for 15-20 minutes until they become plump. Strain and reserve the soaking liquid.
2. Prepare Quail:
- Preheat the grill to medium-high heat. Season the quail with salt and black pepper.
- In a skillet, heat olive oil over medium heat. Add minced garlic and sauté until fragrant.
- Add the soaked porcini mushrooms and cook for 2-3 minutes. Stir in fresh thyme leaves and remove from heat.
3. Grill Quail:
- Place seasoned quail on the preheated grill. Grill each side for 5-7 minutes, or until the quail is cooked through and has a smoky flavor.
- Brush the quail with the porcini and thyme mixture during the last few minutes of grilling.
4. Prepare Polenta:
- In a saucepan, bring the broth and milk to a simmer. Gradually whisk in the polenta, stirring continuously to avoid lumps.
- Cook the polenta over low heat, stirring frequently, until it thickens. Add Parmesan cheese, salt, and black pepper to taste.
5. Serve:
- Plate the wood-grilled quail on a bed of creamy polenta. Drizzle any remaining porcini and thyme mixture over the quail.
- Garnish with fresh thyme leaves and serve immediately.

Nutrition Information:
Per Serving
- Calories: 480
- Protein: 32g
- Carbohydrates: 45g
- Fiber: 5g
- Fat: 18g
- Saturated Fat: 5g

- Cholesterol: 100mg
- Sodium: 900mg

Elevate your culinary skills with this Wood-Grilled Quail with Porcini and Polenta, a tribute to the exceptional flavors found at Nancy Silverton's Mozza. Enjoy the symphony of textures and tastes that make Mozza a culinary destination, right at your own dining table.

18. Shaved Brussels Sprouts Salad with Pecorino and Lemon

Inspired by the culinary brilliance of Nancy Silverton's Mozza restaurant, this Shaved Brussels Sprouts Salad with Pecorino and Lemon is a delightful blend of freshness and zesty flavors. The dish captures the essence of Mozza's commitment to quality ingredients and inventive combinations. Shaved Brussels sprouts provide a crisp base, while the sharpness of Pecorino and the brightness of lemon elevate this salad to a symphony of tastes.

Serving: 4 servings
Preparation Time: 15 minutes
Ready Time: 15 minutes

Ingredients:
- 1 pound Brussels sprouts, trimmed and thinly shaved
- 1/2 cup Pecorino Romano cheese, shaved
- 1/4 cup pine nuts, toasted
- Zest of 1 lemon
- 2 tablespoons fresh lemon juice
- 3 tablespoons extra-virgin olive oil
- Salt and black pepper, to taste
- 2 tablespoons fresh parsley, chopped (for garnish)

Instructions:
1. Prepare Brussels Sprouts: Trim the ends of the Brussels sprouts and remove any damaged outer leaves. Using a sharp knife or a mandolin, thinly shave the Brussels sprouts and place them in a large mixing bowl.

2. Toast Pine Nuts: In a dry skillet over medium heat, toast the pine nuts until they are golden brown and fragrant. Keep an eye on them, as they can burn quickly. Once toasted, set aside.
3. Shave Pecorino: Using a vegetable peeler or a cheese slicer, shave thin pieces of Pecorino Romano cheese.
4. Make Dressing: In a small bowl, whisk together the lemon zest, lemon juice, and extra-virgin olive oil. Season with salt and black pepper to taste.
5. Combine Ingredients: Pour the dressing over the shaved Brussels sprouts in the mixing bowl. Add the shaved Pecorino and toasted pine nuts. Toss the ingredients together until well coated with the dressing.
6. Garnish and Serve: Sprinkle fresh parsley over the salad for a burst of color and added freshness. Serve immediately, and enjoy the vibrant flavors of this Shaved Brussels Sprouts Salad.

Nutrition Information:
(Per serving)
- Calories: 220
- Total Fat: 18g
- Saturated Fat: 4g
- Cholesterol: 10mg
- Sodium: 180mg
- Total Carbohydrates: 10g
- Dietary Fiber: 4g
- Sugars: 2g
- Protein: 7g

Note: Nutrition information is approximate and may vary based on specific ingredients used.

19. White Clam Pizza with Garlic and Chili

Indulge in the culinary magic inspired by the iconic Nancy Silverton's Mozza restaurant with this exquisite White Clam Pizza with Garlic and Chili recipe. This dish embodies the sophistication and flavor nuances characteristic of Mozza's menu. The briny essence of fresh clams, the aromatic allure of garlic, and the subtle heat of chili create a symphony of tastes that will transport you straight to the heart of Mozza's culinary experience.

Serving: Makes 1 large pizza (approximately 8 slices)
Preparation Time: 20 minutes
Ready Time: 30 minutes

Ingredients:
- 1 pound pizza dough, at room temperature
- 2 tablespoons olive oil
- 4 cloves garlic, thinly sliced
- 1/2 teaspoon red chili flakes (adjust to taste)
- 1 cup shredded mozzarella cheese
- 1 cup fresh clams, cleaned and shucked
- 2 tablespoons fresh parsley, chopped
- Salt and black pepper to taste
- Cornmeal or flour for dusting

Instructions:
1. Preheat the Oven:
Preheat your oven to the highest temperature it can reach, typically around 475°F (245°C). If you have a pizza stone, place it in the oven during preheating.
2. Prepare the Dough:
Dust your work surface with cornmeal or flour. Roll out the pizza dough to your desired thickness, ensuring it fits the size of your pizza stone or baking sheet.
3. Sauté Garlic and Chili:
In a small pan, heat the olive oil over medium heat. Add the sliced garlic and red chili flakes, sautéing until the garlic becomes fragrant and golden. Remove from heat.
4. Assemble the Pizza:
Place the rolled-out dough on a pizza peel or a parchment paper-lined baking sheet. Brush the dough with the garlic-infused olive oil. Sprinkle half of the mozzarella evenly over the dough. Distribute the shucked clams evenly, and then add the remaining mozzarella on top.
5. Bake the Pizza:
If using a pizza stone, carefully transfer the pizza onto the preheated stone in the oven. Bake for about 12-15 minutes or until the crust is golden and the cheese is bubbly and slightly browned.
6. Finish and Garnish:

Remove the pizza from the oven and sprinkle with fresh parsley. Season with salt and black pepper to taste.
7. Serve:
Allow the pizza to cool for a few minutes before slicing. Serve slices on a wooden board for a rustic touch.

Nutrition Information:
(Per slice, based on 8 slices)
- Calories: Approximately 250
- Total Fat: 10g
- Saturated Fat: 4g
- Cholesterol: 30mg
- Sodium: 600mg
- Total Carbohydrates: 30g
- Dietary Fiber: 1g
- Sugars: 1g
- Protein: 12g

Indulge in this savory White Clam Pizza with Garlic and Chili, a tribute to the culinary excellence of Nancy Silverton's Mozza restaurant. This dish is a perfect blend of simplicity and sophistication, capturing the essence of Mozza's renowned flavors. Enjoy the journey through each bite!

20. Grilled Radicchio with Balsamic and Gorgonzola

Indulge in the tantalizing flavors of Nancy Silverton's Mozza restaurant with this exquisite recipe for Grilled Radicchio with Balsamic and Gorgonzola. Elevate your culinary experience by combining the bold bitterness of radicchio with the rich sweetness of balsamic glaze and the creamy tang of Gorgonzola. This dish pays homage to the restaurant's commitment to simple yet sophisticated Italian-inspired cuisine.

Serving: 4 servings
Preparation Time: 15 minutes
Ready Time: 25 minutes

Ingredients:
- 2 large heads of radicchio, quartered

- 2 tablespoons olive oil
- Salt and pepper to taste
- 1/4 cup balsamic glaze
- 1/2 cup crumbled Gorgonzola cheese
- Chopped fresh parsley for garnish (optional)

Instructions:

1. Preheat the Grill:
- Preheat your grill to medium-high heat. Make sure the grates are clean and lightly oiled.
2. Prepare the Radicchio:
- Cut each radicchio head into quarters, ensuring that the core remains intact to hold the leaves together.
3. Season with Olive Oil, Salt, and Pepper:
- Drizzle the radicchio quarters with olive oil, ensuring each piece is well-coated. Sprinkle with salt and pepper to taste.
4. Grill the Radicchio:
- Place the radicchio quarters on the preheated grill. Grill for about 3-4 minutes per side or until the leaves are slightly charred and the radicchio is tender.
5. Drizzle with Balsamic Glaze:
- Transfer the grilled radicchio to a serving platter. Drizzle the balsamic glaze over the top, ensuring each piece is generously coated.
6. Add Gorgonzola Cheese:
- Sprinkle the crumbled Gorgonzola cheese over the grilled radicchio while it's still warm. The heat will slightly melt the cheese, creating a luscious texture.
7. Garnish and Serve:
- If desired, garnish with chopped fresh parsley for a burst of color and freshness. Serve the Grilled Radicchio with Balsamic and Gorgonzola immediately.

Nutrition Information:

(Per Serving)
- Calories: XXX
- Total Fat: XXg
- Saturated Fat: XXg
- Cholesterol: XXmg
- Sodium: XXXmg
- Total Carbohydrates: XXg

- Dietary Fiber: XXg
- Sugars: XXg
- Protein: XXg

Embrace the bold and distinctive flavors of Mozza's menu with this Grilled Radicchio dish. It's a delightful combination of bitter, sweet, and savory that will leave your taste buds craving for more. Enjoy the taste of Italy in the comfort of your own home.

21. Butternut Squash Pizza with Crème Fraîche and Bacon

Indulge in the culinary artistry inspired by Nancy Silverton's Mozza restaurant with our Butternut Squash Pizza featuring the rich creaminess of Crème Fraîche and the savory crunch of bacon. This unique twist on a classic pizza promises a harmonious blend of flavors that will elevate your pizza night to new heights. Unleash your inner pizza connoisseur and savor the magic of Mozza in the comfort of your home.

Serving: 4 servings
Preparation time: 20 minutes
Ready time: 30 minutes

Ingredients:
- 1 pound pizza dough (store-bought or homemade)
- 1 small butternut squash, peeled, seeded, and thinly sliced
- 1 cup Crème Fraîche
- 6 slices of bacon, cooked and crumbled
- 1 cup shredded mozzarella cheese
- 2 tablespoons olive oil
- Salt and pepper to taste
- Fresh thyme leaves for garnish

Instructions:
1. Preheat Oven:
Preheat your oven to 475°F (245°C). If you have a pizza stone, place it in the oven to heat.
2. Prepare Butternut Squash:

Peel, seed, and thinly slice the butternut squash. Toss the slices with olive oil, salt, and pepper in a bowl.
3. Roll Out Pizza Dough:
On a floured surface, roll out the pizza dough to your desired thickness. If you have a pizza peel, transfer the rolled-out dough onto it.
4. Assemble Pizza:
Spread a generous layer of Crème Fraîche over the rolled-out dough. Arrange the butternut squash slices evenly. Sprinkle the shredded mozzarella over the squash, and scatter the crumbled bacon on top.
5. Bake the Pizza:
If using a pizza stone, carefully transfer the pizza onto the preheated stone in the oven. Otherwise, place the pizza on a baking sheet. Bake for 12-15 minutes or until the crust is golden and the toppings are bubbly and slightly browned.
6. Garnish and Serve:
Once out of the oven, sprinkle fresh thyme leaves over the hot pizza. Allow it to cool for a few minutes before slicing.

Nutrition Information:
(Per Serving)
- Calories: 450
- Protein: 12g
- Carbohydrates: 50g
- Fat: 22g
- Saturated Fat: 9g
- Cholesterol: 45mg
- Sodium: 700mg
- Fiber: 5g
- Sugar: 5g

Elevate your pizza experience with the unique combination of butternut squash, Crème Fraîche, and bacon—a culinary masterpiece inspired by the spirit of Nancy Silverton's Mozza restaurant. Enjoy the perfect balance of flavors in every delightful bite!

22. Wood-Roasted Mussels with White Wine and Garlic

Indulge in the rustic flavors reminiscent of Nancy Silverton's Mozza restaurant with these wood-roasted mussels. The combination of succulent mussels, aromatic garlic, and the delicate touch of white wine creates a dish that encapsulates the essence of coastal Italian cuisine.

Serving: Serves: 4
Preparation Time: 15 minutes
Ready Time: Cook: 15 minutes
Total: 30 minutes

Ingredients:
- 2 pounds fresh mussels, cleaned and debearded
- 4 tablespoons extra-virgin olive oil
- 4 cloves garlic, thinly sliced
- 1 cup dry white wine
- 2 tablespoons chopped fresh parsley
- Salt and freshly ground black pepper, to taste
- Crusty bread, for serving

Instructions:
1. Preheat the Grill: Prepare a wood-fired grill for medium-high heat.
2. Prepare the Mussels: Rinse the mussels under cold water, scrubbing away any debris. Discard any mussels that are open or broken.
3. Sauté Garlic: In a large skillet or cast-iron pan, heat the olive oil over medium heat. Add the sliced garlic and sauté for 1-2 minutes until fragrant, being careful not to let it brown.
4. Add Mussels and Wine: Increase the heat to high and add the cleaned mussels to the skillet. Pour in the white wine and cover the skillet with a lid. Let the mussels cook for 5-7 minutes, shaking the pan occasionally, until the mussels have opened.
5. Season and Garnish: Once the mussels have opened, remove the skillet from heat. Season with salt and pepper to taste. Sprinkle with chopped fresh parsley for a burst of color and flavor.
6. Grill the Mussels: Transfer the skillet to the preheated wood-fired grill. Grill for 2-3 minutes, allowing the smoky flavors to infuse into the mussels.
7. Serve: Remove the skillet from the grill and serve the wood-roasted mussels directly from the pan. Accompany with crusty bread to soak up the delicious broth.

Nutrition Information
Note: Nutrition information may vary depending on specific ingredients used and serving sizes.
- Calories: Approximately 220 per serving
- Fat: 10g
- Carbohydrates: 6g
- Protein: 18g
- Sodium: 650mg
- Fiber: 0.5g

Enjoy the delightful aroma and flavors of these wood-roasted mussels, perfect for a cozy dinner or a delightful appetizer to share among friends and family.

23. Prosciutto and Burrata Crostini with Balsamic Glaze

Indulge in the delightful flavors of Mozza restaurant with these Prosciutto and Burrata Crostini with Balsamic Glaze. This appetizer embodies the essence of Italian cuisine, combining the richness of burrata cheese, the saltiness of prosciutto, and the sweetness of balsamic glaze atop crisp crostini.

Serving: Makes 12 crostini
Preparation time: 15 minutes
Ready time: 20 minutes

Ingredients:
- 1 French baguette, sliced into ½-inch thick rounds
- 8 ounces burrata cheese
- 6-8 slices prosciutto
- 1/4 cup balsamic glaze
- 2 tablespoons extra virgin olive oil
- Fresh basil leaves, for garnish
- Salt and pepper to taste

Instructions:
1. Preheat the Oven: Preheat your oven to 375°F (190°C).

2. Prepare the Crostini: Place the baguette slices on a baking sheet and brush each slice lightly with olive oil. Season with a pinch of salt and pepper. Bake in the preheated oven for 8-10 minutes or until the crostini turns golden and crisp. Remove from the oven and let them cool slightly.
3. Assemble the Crostini: Cut or tear the burrata into small pieces. Place a spoonful of burrata on each crostini slice. Tear the prosciutto into smaller pieces and drape it over the burrata.
4. Drizzle with Balsamic Glaze: Generously drizzle the balsamic glaze over the assembled crostini.
5. Garnish and Serve: Top each crostini with fresh basil leaves for a burst of aroma and flavor. Arrange the crostini on a platter and serve immediately.

Nutrition Information: (per crostini)
- Calories: 120
- Total Fat: 7g
- Saturated Fat: 3g
- Cholesterol: 15mg
- Sodium: 230mg
- Total Carbohydrate: 9g
- Dietary Fiber: 1g
- Sugars: 2g
- Protein: 6g

These Prosciutto and Burrata Crostini are a perfect blend of textures and flavors, ideal for entertaining or as an elegant starter for a meal. Enjoy the sophistication of Mozza's menu in the comfort of your own home!

24. Wood-Grilled Swordfish with Caper and Olive Relish

Drawing inspiration from Nancy Silverton's Mozza restaurant, this wood-grilled swordfish dish with a zesty caper and olive relish is a celebration of flavors and textures. The robust taste of the swordfish pairs beautifully with the tangy relish, making it a delightful culinary experience reminiscent of Mozza's vibrant menu.

Serving: This recipe serves 4.
Preparation Time: - 15 minutes for preparation

- 30 minutes for marinating (optional)
Ready Time: Approximately 30 minutes

Ingredients:
- 4 swordfish steaks (6 ounces each)
- 1/4 cup extra-virgin olive oil
- 2 tablespoons fresh lemon juice
- 2 cloves garlic, minced
- Salt and pepper to taste
- 1/4 cup chopped fresh parsley
- 1/4 cup chopped pitted green olives
- 2 tablespoons capers, drained and chopped
- 2 tablespoons finely chopped red onion
- 1 tablespoon red wine vinegar
- Lemon wedges for serving

Instructions:
1. Prepare the Swordfish:
- Preheat a wood grill or a grill pan over medium-high heat.
- In a small bowl, whisk together 2 tablespoons of olive oil, lemon juice, minced garlic, salt, and pepper.
- Pat dry the swordfish steaks and brush them with the olive oil mixture. Let them marinate for 30 minutes if time allows.
2. Make the Relish:
- In another bowl, combine the chopped parsley, olives, capers, red onion, remaining olive oil, and red wine vinegar. Mix well and set aside.
3. Grill the Swordfish:
- Oil the grill grates lightly. Place the swordfish steaks on the grill and cook for about 4-5 minutes on each side or until the fish is cooked through and has nice grill marks.
4. Serve:
- Transfer the grilled swordfish steaks to a serving platter.
- Spoon the prepared caper and olive relish over the swordfish.
- Garnish with additional chopped parsley if desired.
- Serve hot with lemon wedges on the side.

Nutrition Information (per serving):
- Calories: Approximately 350
- Protein: 35g
- Fat: 20g

- Carbohydrates: 4g
- Fiber: 1g
- Sodium: 700mg
- Note: Nutritional values may vary depending on portion sizes and specific ingredients used.

Enjoy this Wood-Grilled Swordfish with Caper and Olive Relish inspired by the vibrant flavors of Nancy Silverton's Mozza restaurant!

25. Caprese Salad with Heirloom Tomatoes and Basil

Indulge in the vibrant flavors of Mozza restaurant with this delightful Caprese Salad featuring the finest heirloom tomatoes and fragrant basil. Inspired by the culinary genius of Nancy Silverton, this dish pays homage to the simplicity and quality ingredients that define Mozza's menu. Elevate your dining experience with the freshness of seasonal produce and the classic combination of tomatoes, mozzarella, and basil.

Serving: 4 servings
Preparation Time: 15 minutes
Ready Time: 15 minutes

Ingredients:
- 4 large heirloom tomatoes, sliced
- 1 pound fresh mozzarella cheese, sliced
- 1 bunch fresh basil leaves
- 1/4 cup extra-virgin olive oil
- 2 tablespoons balsamic glaze
- Salt and pepper to taste

Instructions:
1. Prepare the Tomatoes:
- Wash and dry the heirloom tomatoes. Slice them into 1/4-inch thick rounds.
2. Slice the Mozzarella:
- Cut the fresh mozzarella into slices of similar thickness to the tomatoes.
3. Assemble the Salad:

- On a serving platter, alternate layers of tomato slices and mozzarella. Tuck fresh basil leaves between the layers.
4. Drizzle with Olive Oil:
- Drizzle extra-virgin olive oil over the assembled salad, ensuring each layer is lightly coated.
5. Season and Garnish:
- Sprinkle salt and pepper over the salad to taste. Drizzle the balsamic glaze over the top for a sweet and tangy finish.
6. Serve:
- Serve the Caprese Salad immediately to enjoy the peak freshness of the ingredients.

Nutrition Information:
- *Note: Nutrition values are approximate and may vary based on specific ingredients used.*
- Serving Size: 1/4 of the recipe
- Calories: 350
- Total Fat: 28g
- Saturated Fat: 12g
- Trans Fat: 0g
- Cholesterol: 60mg
- Sodium: 450mg
- Total Carbohydrates: 8g
- Dietary Fiber: 2g
- Sugars: 5g
- Protein: 18g
- Vitamin D: 0%
- Calcium: 40%
- Iron: 6%
- Potassium: 15%

Note:

Feel free to customize the salad with additional ingredients such as pine nuts, cherry tomatoes, or a sprinkle of Parmesan cheese for a unique twist on this classic Mozza-inspired dish. Enjoy the vibrant colors and flavors of this Caprese Salad that embodies the essence of Nancy Silverton's culinary mastery.

26. Margherita Pizza with Salami and Calabrian Chili

Indulge in the culinary magic inspired by Nancy Silverton's iconic Mozza restaurant with our twist on the classic Margherita Pizza. Elevating this timeless favorite, we've added a tantalizing kick with slices of savory salami and the bold heat of Calabrian chili. Immerse yourself in the rich flavors and textures that pay homage to Mozza's unparalleled dining experience.

Serving: Makes 1 large pizza (8 slices)
Preparation Time: 15 minutes
Ready Time: 25 minutes

Ingredients:
- 1 pizza dough (store-bought or homemade)
- 1/2 cup pizza sauce
- 1 1/2 cups fresh mozzarella, sliced
- 1/4 cup grated Parmesan cheese
- 4 ounces thinly sliced salami
- 1-2 tablespoons Calabrian chili, finely chopped
- Fresh basil leaves, for garnish
- Olive oil, for drizzling
- Flour or cornmeal, for dusting

Instructions:
1. Preheat the Oven:
Preheat your oven to the highest temperature it can reach (usually around 475-500°F or 245-260°C). If you have a pizza stone, place it in the oven during preheating.
2. Prepare the Dough:
Roll out the pizza dough on a lightly floured surface, shaping it into a round or rectangular form, depending on your preference.
3. Assemble the Pizza:
Transfer the rolled-out dough to a pizza peel or an inverted baking sheet dusted with flour or cornmeal. Spread the pizza sauce evenly over the dough, leaving a small border around the edges. Arrange the fresh mozzarella slices, followed by the salami.
4. Add the Heat:

Sprinkle the Calabrian chili evenly over the pizza for that extra punch of spice.
5. Bake to Perfection:
If using a pizza stone, carefully transfer the pizza onto the preheated stone in the oven. If not, simply place the baking sheet with the pizza directly in the oven. Bake for about 12-15 minutes or until the crust is golden and the cheese is bubbly and slightly browned.
6. Garnish and Serve:
Remove the pizza from the oven, drizzle with olive oil, and garnish with fresh basil leaves. Allow it to cool for a few minutes before slicing.
7. Slice and Enjoy:
Slice the Margherita Pizza with Salami and Calabrian Chili into 8 pieces and savor the perfect blend of classic and bold flavors.

Nutrition Information:
Note: Nutrition information is approximate and may vary based on specific ingredients and portion sizes.
- Calories per slice: 250
- Total Fat: 12g
- Saturated Fat: 5g
- Cholesterol: 25mg
- Sodium: 600mg
- Total Carbohydrates: 25g
- Dietary Fiber: 1g
- Sugars: 2g
- Protein: 12g
Adjust serving size and ingredient quantities for personalized nutrition information.

27. Fried Squash Blossoms with Ricotta and Lemon Zest

Indulge your palate in the culinary symphony inspired by the iconic Mozza restaurant, crafted by the renowned Nancy Silverton. One of the delicacies that captures the essence of Mozza's innovation is the Fried Squash Blossoms with Ricotta and Lemon Zest. This dish harmoniously combines the delicate crunch of fried squash blossoms with the creamy richness of ricotta and the zesty brightness of lemon, creating a sensation that lingers on the taste buds.

Serving: 4 servings
Preparation Time: 15 minutes
Ready Time: 30 minutes

Ingredients:
- 12 fresh squash blossoms
- 1 cup ricotta cheese
- Zest of 1 lemon
- 1 cup all-purpose flour
- 1 cup sparkling water (chilled)
- 1/2 teaspoon salt
- Vegetable oil for frying
- Lemon wedges for serving
- Salt and pepper to taste

Instructions:
1. Prepare the Squash Blossoms:
- Gently open each squash blossom and remove the stamen from inside. Be careful not to tear the delicate petals.
- Rinse the blossoms under cold water and pat them dry with paper towels.
2. Make the Ricotta Filling:
- In a bowl, combine ricotta cheese and lemon zest. Mix well until the lemon zest is evenly distributed.
3. Fill the Squash Blossoms:
- Using a small spoon, carefully stuff each blossom with the ricotta mixture. Be sure not to overfill, as the blossoms will be dipped in batter before frying.
4. Prepare the Batter:
- In a mixing bowl, whisk together the all-purpose flour, chilled sparkling water, and salt until you achieve a smooth, lump-free batter.
5. Fry the Squash Blossoms:
- Heat vegetable oil in a deep pan or fryer to 350°F (175°C).
- Dip each stuffed blossom into the batter, ensuring an even coating, and carefully place them in the hot oil.
- Fry until golden brown, about 2-3 minutes per side.

- Use a slotted spoon to remove the fried blossoms and place them on a paper towel to absorb any excess oil.
6. Season and Serve:
- Sprinkle the fried squash blossoms with salt and pepper to taste.
- Serve immediately with lemon wedges on the side for a refreshing citrus kick.

Nutrition Information:
Note: Nutritional values are approximate and may vary based on specific ingredients used.
- Calories per serving: 240
- Total Fat: 12g
- Saturated Fat: 6g
- Cholesterol: 30mg
- Sodium: 380mg
- Total Carbohydrates: 25g
- Dietary Fiber: 2g
- Sugars: 2g
- Protein: 10g

Elevate your home cooking with this Mozza-inspired masterpiece, where the delicate crispiness of the squash blossoms meets the velvety embrace of ricotta, creating a culinary experience that echoes the brilliance of Nancy Silverton's creations.

28. Grilled Shrimp with Saffron Aioli and Lemon

Indulge your taste buds in a culinary journey inspired by the renowned Nancy Silverton's Mozza restaurant with this exquisite recipe for Grilled Shrimp with Saffron Aioli and Lemon. The dish effortlessly combines the succulence of grilled shrimp with the rich, aromatic flavors of saffron-infused aioli, all brightened by a touch of zesty lemon. Elevate your dining experience with this sophisticated yet simple creation that captures the essence of Mozza's exceptional cuisine.

Serving: 4 servings
Preparation Time: 15 minutes
Ready Time: 30 minutes

Ingredients:
- 1 pound large shrimp, peeled and deveined
- 2 tablespoons olive oil
- Salt and black pepper to taste
- Wooden skewers, soaked in water for 30 minutes

For the Saffron Aioli:
- 1 cup mayonnaise
- 2 cloves garlic, minced
- 1 teaspoon Dijon mustard
- 1 teaspoon saffron threads, soaked in 1 tablespoon warm water
- 1 tablespoon lemon juice
- Salt and black pepper to taste

For Garnish:
- Fresh parsley, chopped
- Lemon wedges

Instructions:

1. Preheat the Grill:

Preheat your grill to medium-high heat.

2. Prepare the Shrimp:

In a bowl, toss the shrimp with olive oil, salt, and black pepper. Thread the shrimp onto the soaked wooden skewers.

3. Grill the Shrimp:

Place the skewers on the preheated grill and cook for 2-3 minutes per side or until the shrimp are opaque and slightly charred.

4. Make the Saffron Aioli:

In a small bowl, whisk together mayonnaise, minced garlic, Dijon mustard, soaked saffron threads with water, lemon juice, salt, and black pepper. Adjust the seasoning to taste.

5. Serve:

Arrange the grilled shrimp on a serving platter. Drizzle the saffron aioli over the shrimp and garnish with chopped fresh parsley. Serve with lemon wedges on the side.

Nutrition Information:

(Per serving)
- Calories: 320
- Protein: 25g
- Carbohydrates: 4g
- Fat: 22g

- Saturated Fat: 3g
- Cholesterol: 220mg
- Sodium: 550mg
- Fiber: 0g
- Sugar: 1g

Indulge in the vibrant flavors of Mozza's menu with this Grilled Shrimp dish, a perfect blend of simplicity and sophistication that is sure to leave a lasting impression on your palate.

29. Garganelli with Duck Ragu and Parmesan

Indulge in the rich and tantalizing flavors inspired by the renowned Nancy Silverton's Mozza restaurant with our Garganelli with Duck Ragu and Parmesan recipe. This dish perfectly captures the essence of the restaurant's commitment to exquisite Italian cuisine. The tender shreds of duck, slow-cooked in a flavorful ragu, are paired with the delightful bite of garganelli pasta and finished with a generous shower of Parmesan. Prepare to elevate your dining experience with this sumptuous creation that pays homage to the culinary excellence of Mozza.

Serving: 4 servings
Preparation Time: 20 minutes
Ready Time: 2 hours (includes cooking time)

Ingredients:
- 1 lb garganelli pasta
- 2 duck legs, confit
- 1 onion, finely chopped
- 2 carrots, diced
- 2 celery stalks, diced
- 3 cloves garlic, minced
- 1 cup red wine
- 2 cans (14 oz each) crushed tomatoes
- 2 cups chicken broth
- 1 teaspoon dried thyme
- 1 teaspoon dried oregano
- Salt and black pepper to taste
- 1/2 cup Parmesan cheese, grated

- Fresh parsley, chopped (for garnish)

Instructions:

1. Prepare the Duck: In a large pan, gently heat the duck confit until the skin is crispy. Remove the skin, shred the meat, and set aside.
2. Make the Ragu: In the same pan, sauté the chopped onion, carrots, celery, and minced garlic until softened. Add the shredded duck to the vegetables and stir well.
3. Add Liquids: Pour in the red wine, scraping the bottom of the pan to deglaze it. Allow the wine to reduce by half. Add crushed tomatoes, chicken broth, dried thyme, dried oregano, salt, and black pepper. Bring the mixture to a simmer, then reduce the heat and let it cook slowly for at least 1.5 to 2 hours, allowing the flavors to meld.
4. Cook the Pasta: In a separate pot, cook the garganelli pasta according to package instructions until al dente. Drain and set aside.
5. Combine and Serve: Once the ragu has thickened, combine it with the cooked garganelli pasta. Toss until the pasta is evenly coated with the duck ragu.
6. Finish with Parmesan: Sprinkle the grated Parmesan over the pasta and ragu, stirring gently to incorporate. Allow it to melt and meld into the dish.
7. Garnish and Serve: Serve the Garganelli with Duck Ragu and Parmesan hot, garnished with fresh chopped parsley for a burst of color and added freshness.

Nutrition Information:

(Per Serving)

- Calories: 600
- Protein: 28g
- Fat: 15g
- Carbohydrates: 80g
- Fiber: 8g
- Sugar: 12g
- Sodium: 800mg

Immerse yourself in the culinary brilliance of Mozza with this Garganelli with Duck Ragu and Parmesan, a dish that marries tradition with innovation on every plate.

30. Radicchio and Endive Salad with Gorgonzola and Walnuts

Indulge in the vibrant flavors and textures of the Radicchio and Endive Salad with Gorgonzola and Walnuts, inspired by the culinary genius of Nancy Silverton's Mozza restaurant. This salad is a delightful symphony of bitter radicchio, crisp endive, creamy Gorgonzola, and crunchy walnuts. Each bite is a harmonious blend of contrasting elements that showcases the restaurant's commitment to exquisite taste and balance.

Serving: 4 servings
Preparation Time: 15 minutes
Ready Time: 15 minutes

Ingredients:
- 1 head radicchio, thinly sliced
- 2 heads endive, sliced into thin rounds
- 1 cup Gorgonzola cheese, crumbled
- 1 cup walnuts, toasted and chopped
- 1/4 cup extra-virgin olive oil
- 2 tablespoons red wine vinegar
- 1 teaspoon Dijon mustard
- Salt and black pepper to taste

Instructions:
1. In a large bowl, combine the sliced radicchio and endive.
2. In a small bowl, whisk together the olive oil, red wine vinegar, Dijon mustard, salt, and black pepper to create the dressing.
3. Drizzle the dressing over the radicchio and endive, tossing gently to coat the greens evenly.
4. Sprinkle the crumbled Gorgonzola and toasted walnuts over the salad, distributing them evenly.
5. Toss the salad one more time, ensuring that the ingredients are well combined.
6. Allow the salad to sit for a few minutes to let the flavors meld.
7. Serve the Radicchio and Endive Salad with Gorgonzola and Walnuts on individual plates, appreciating the vibrant colors and rich textures.

Nutrition Information:

(Per serving)
- Calories: 320
- Total Fat: 27g
- Saturated Fat: 7g
- Cholesterol: 20mg
- Sodium: 450mg
- Total Carbohydrates: 10g
- Dietary Fiber: 4g
- Sugars: 3g
- Protein: 11g

Elevate your dining experience with this elegant salad that captures the essence of Nancy Silverton's Mozza restaurant, where culinary artistry meets bold flavors.

31. Margherita Pizza with Cherry Tomatoes and Arugula

Indulge in the quintessential flavors of Italy with this Margherita Pizza topped with vibrant cherry tomatoes and peppery arugula. Inspired by the renowned Mozza restaurant, this recipe embodies the essence of simple yet exquisite Italian cuisine.

Serving: 2-4 people
Preparation time: 1 hour
Ready time: 2 hours (including dough resting time)

Ingredients:
- 1 pound pizza dough (store-bought or homemade)
- 1/2 cup marinara sauce
- 8 ounces fresh mozzarella, sliced
- 1 cup cherry tomatoes, halved
- 1 cup fresh arugula
- Extra-virgin olive oil
- Salt and pepper to taste
- Fresh basil leaves for garnish (optional)

Instructions:
1. Prepare the Dough:

- If using store-bought dough, allow it to come to room temperature. If making homemade dough, follow your preferred recipe and let it rise according to instructions.
2. Preheat the Oven:
- Place a pizza stone or baking sheet in the oven. Preheat to 475°F (245°C) for at least 30 minutes.
3. Shape the Pizza:
- On a floured surface, stretch or roll out the pizza dough into a round shape, aiming for about 12 inches in diameter.
4. Assemble the Pizza:
- Place the stretched dough onto parchment paper. Spread the marinara sauce evenly over the dough, leaving a small border for the crust.
- Arrange the slices of fresh mozzarella on top of the sauce.
- Scatter the halved cherry tomatoes over the cheese.
5. Bake the Pizza:
- Carefully transfer the parchment paper with the assembled pizza onto the preheated pizza stone or baking sheet in the oven.
- Bake for 12-15 minutes or until the crust is golden brown, and the cheese is bubbly and slightly browned.
6. Finish and Serve:
- Once out of the oven, sprinkle the fresh arugula over the hot pizza.
- Drizzle with a bit of extra-virgin olive oil and season with salt and pepper to taste.
- Garnish with fresh basil leaves if desired.

Nutrition Information: (Per Serving - estimated)
- Calories: 350-400 kcal
- Total Fat: 15-20g
- Saturated Fat: 7-10g
- Carbohydrates: 40-45g
- Fiber: 2-3g
- Protein: 15-20g

The nutritional values may vary based on specific ingredients and portion sizes used.
This delightful Margherita Pizza with Cherry Tomatoes and Arugula serves as a wonderful homage to the flavors found at Nancy Silverton's Mozza, capturing the essence of traditional Italian cuisine in every bite. Enjoy!

32. Wood-Grilled Ribeye with Roasted Mushrooms and Thyme

Inspired by the flavors and quality of Nancy Silverton's renowned Mozza restaurant, this wood-grilled ribeye with roasted mushrooms and thyme embodies the essence of hearty, comforting dining. The rich, smoky flavors from the grill combined with earthy mushrooms and fragrant thyme create a sensational dish that captures the essence of Mozza's culinary excellence.

Serving: 2 servings
Preparation time: 15 minutes
Ready time: 40 minutes

Ingredients:
- 2 boneless ribeye steaks (about 1 inch thick)
- 2 cups mixed mushrooms (such as cremini, shiitake, or oyster), sliced
- 3 tablespoons olive oil
- 3 cloves garlic, minced
- 2 teaspoons fresh thyme leaves, plus extra for garnish
- Salt and black pepper to taste

Instructions:
1. Preheat a wood-fired grill or a regular grill to medium-high heat.
2. Season the ribeye steaks generously with salt and pepper on both sides.
3. In a bowl, toss the sliced mushrooms with 2 tablespoons of olive oil, minced garlic, fresh thyme leaves, salt, and pepper until well coated.
4. Place the seasoned ribeye steaks on the grill and cook for about 4-5 minutes per side for medium-rare doneness, or adjust based on your preferred level of doneness.
5. While the steaks are grilling, spread the seasoned mushrooms on a baking sheet and roast in the oven at 400°F (200°C) for 15-20 minutes until they turn golden brown and tender.
6. As the steaks finish grilling, remove them from the heat and let them rest for 5-10 minutes before slicing.
7. Arrange the sliced ribeye steaks on plates and top generously with the roasted mushrooms. Garnish with extra fresh thyme leaves.
8. Drizzle the remaining tablespoon of olive oil over the dish before serving.

Nutrition Information:
- Calories: Approximately 500 calories per serving
- Protein: 40g
- Carbohydrates: 2g
- Fat: 38g
- Saturated Fat: 10g
- Cholesterol: 120mg
- Sodium: 80mg
- Fiber: 1g
- Sugar: 1g

(Note: Nutritional values are approximate and may vary based on specific ingredients used.)

33. Burrata with Roasted Peppers, Pine Nuts, and Golden Raisins

Indulge in the Mediterranean flavors inspired by Nancy Silverton's Mozza restaurant with this exquisite dish of creamy burrata complemented by the sweetness of roasted peppers, the nuttiness of pine nuts, and the delightful tang of golden raisins. It's a perfect harmony of textures and tastes that will elevate your dining experience.

Serving: This recipe serves 4.
Preparation Time: Preparation time is approximately 15 minutes.
Ready Time: Ready to serve in about 35 minutes.

Ingredients:
- 2 red bell peppers
- 2 yellow bell peppers
- 1 tablespoon olive oil
- Salt and pepper to taste
- 1/4 cup pine nuts, toasted
- 1/4 cup golden raisins
- 2 tablespoons fresh basil leaves, thinly sliced
- 8 ounces burrata cheese
- Balsamic glaze (optional)

Instructions:

1. Preheat the oven to 400°F (200°C).
2. Cut the bell peppers in half lengthwise and remove the seeds and membranes. Place them on a baking sheet, skin side up.
3. Drizzle the peppers with olive oil and season with salt and pepper.
4. Roast the peppers in the preheated oven for 20-25 minutes or until the skins are blistered and lightly charred.
5. Remove the peppers from the oven and place them in a bowl. Cover the bowl with plastic wrap and let them steam for 10 minutes. This will make peeling the skins off easier.
6. Once cooled, peel the skins off the peppers and slice them into thin strips.
7. In a small pan over low heat, toast the pine nuts until they turn golden brown, stirring frequently to avoid burning.
8. In a small bowl, soak the golden raisins in warm water for 5-10 minutes to plump them up. Drain and pat dry.
9. To assemble, arrange the roasted pepper strips on a serving platter.
10. Place the burrata in the center of the peppers.
11. Sprinkle the pine nuts and golden raisins over the peppers and burrata.
12. Garnish with thinly sliced fresh basil leaves.
13. Optionally, drizzle with balsamic glaze for an extra burst of flavor.
14. Serve immediately and enjoy the burst of flavors and textures.

Nutrition Information:

*Note: Nutritional values may vary depending on specific ingredients used and serving sizes.

- Calories: Approximately 250 per serving
- Fat: Approximately 18g
- Carbohydrates: Approximately 14g
- Protein: Approximately 12g
- Fiber: Approximately 2g

Adjust the ingredient amounts and serving sizes according to your dietary needs and preferences.

34. Wood-Roasted Sardines with Fennel and Lemon

Indulge in the rustic charm of wood-roasted sardines, inspired by the culinary magic of Nancy Silverton's iconic Mozza restaurant. This dish captures the essence of Mediterranean flavors, blending the boldness of sardines with the aromatic notes of fennel and the zesty brightness of lemon. A tribute to the culinary prowess of Mozza, this recipe promises a symphony of tastes that will transport you to the heart of Silverton's gastronomic world.

Serving: 4 servings
Preparation Time: 15 minutes
Ready Time: 30 minutes

Ingredients:
- 12 fresh sardines, cleaned and gutted
- 2 fennel bulbs, thinly sliced
- 1 lemon, thinly sliced
- 4 cloves garlic, minced
- 1/4 cup fresh parsley, chopped
- 1/3 cup extra-virgin olive oil
- Salt and pepper, to taste
- Wooden skewers, soaked in water for 30 minutes

Instructions:
1. Preheat the Wood-Fired Oven or Grill:
- If using a wood-fired oven, light the wood and let it burn until you have a bed of hot embers. If using a grill, preheat it to medium-high heat.
2. Prepare the Sardines:
- Make sure the sardines are cleaned and gutted. Season them with salt and pepper, inside and out.
3. Create Sardine Skewers:
- Thread the sardines onto the soaked wooden skewers. This will make them easier to handle on the grill or in the wood-fired oven.
4. Assemble the Dish:
- In a bowl, combine the sliced fennel, lemon slices, minced garlic, and chopped parsley. Drizzle with olive oil and season with salt and pepper. Toss to coat evenly.
5. Wood-Roast the Sardines:
- Place the sardine skewers on the grill or in the wood-fired oven. Cook for about 5-7 minutes, turning occasionally, until the sardines are cooked through and have a nice char.

6. Serve:
- Arrange the wood-roasted sardines on a platter and top with the fennel, lemon, and garlic mixture. Drizzle with additional olive oil if desired. Garnish with fresh parsley.

Nutrition Information:
Note: Nutritional values are approximate and may vary based on specific ingredients used.
- Calories: 320 per serving
- Protein: 22g
- Fat: 24g
- Carbohydrates: 8g
- Fiber: 3g
- Sugar: 2g
- Sodium: 480mg

Indulge in the robust flavors of wood-roasted sardines with fennel and lemon—a culinary journey inspired by the timeless elegance of Nancy Silverton's Mozza restaurant. This dish is a testament to the harmonious blend of fresh, quality ingredients and the art of wood-fired cooking.

35. Margherita Pizza with Eggplant and Ricotta

Indulge your taste buds in a culinary journey inspired by the renowned Nancy Silverton's Mozza restaurant with our twist on the classic Margherita Pizza. Elevate the traditional flavors by adding roasted eggplant and creamy ricotta, creating a delightful fusion that is both sophisticated and comforting. This recipe promises a symphony of textures and tastes that will transport you to the heart of Mozza's exceptional culinary experience.

Serving: 4 servings
Preparation Time: 20 minutes
Ready Time: 30 minutes

Ingredients:
- 1 pound pizza dough, at room temperature
- 1 cup marinara sauce
- 1 large eggplant, thinly sliced

- 1 cup ricotta cheese
- 1 1/2 cups fresh mozzarella, sliced
- 1/4 cup fresh basil leaves, torn
- 2 tablespoons extra-virgin olive oil
- Salt and black pepper to taste
- Cornmeal or flour for dusting

Instructions:
1. Preheat the Oven:
Preheat your oven to 475°F (245°C). If you have a pizza stone, place it in the oven to heat.
2. Prepare the Eggplant:
Lay out the eggplant slices on a baking sheet. Drizzle with olive oil, season with salt and pepper, and roast in the preheated oven for about 10 minutes, or until the slices are tender and slightly golden.
3. Roll Out the Dough:
Dust your work surface with flour or cornmeal. Roll out the pizza dough to your desired thickness. If you have a pizza peel, transfer the rolled-out dough onto it.
4. Assemble the Pizza:
Spread the marinara sauce evenly over the rolled-out dough, leaving a small border for the crust. Arrange the roasted eggplant slices on top. Dot the pizza with spoonfuls of ricotta and distribute the fresh mozzarella slices evenly.
5. Bake the Pizza:
If using a pizza stone, carefully transfer the pizza onto the hot stone in the oven. Bake for 12-15 minutes or until the crust is golden and the cheese is bubbly and slightly browned.
6. Finish and Serve:
Once out of the oven, sprinkle torn fresh basil leaves over the hot pizza. Drizzle with a bit of extra-virgin olive oil. Allow the pizza to cool for a few minutes before slicing.

Nutrition Information:
Per Serving:
- Calories: 450
- Total Fat: 20g
- Saturated Fat: 8g
- Cholesterol: 35mg
- Sodium: 900mg

- Total Carbohydrates: 50g
- Dietary Fiber: 5g
- Sugars: 6g
- Protein: 15g

Elevate your pizza night with this Margherita Pizza featuring the unique flavors of eggplant and ricotta—a true homage to the culinary excellence of Nancy Silverton's Mozza restaurant. Enjoy!

36. Grilled Artichokes with Lemon and Garlic Aioli

Indulge in the exquisite flavors inspired by the renowned menu of Nancy Silverton's Mozza restaurant with these Grilled Artichokes featuring a zesty Lemon and Garlic Aioli. A delightful harmony of smoky grilled artichokes and a creamy aioli, this dish captures the essence of Mozza's culinary artistry. Perfect as an appetizer or a side, these grilled artichokes are a testament to the restaurant's dedication to exceptional taste and quality ingredients.

Serving: 4 servings
Preparation Time: 20 minutes
Ready Time: 40 minutes

Ingredients:
- 4 large artichokes
- 2 lemons, halved
- 3 tablespoons olive oil
- Salt and black pepper to taste

For Lemon and Garlic Aioli:
- 1 cup mayonnaise
- 2 cloves garlic, minced
- Zest of 1 lemon
- 2 tablespoons lemon juice
- Salt and black pepper to taste

Instructions:
1. Prepare the Artichokes:
- Trim the top inch off the artichokes and cut off the stems.
- Cut the artichokes in half lengthwise.

- Use a spoon to scrape out the fuzzy choke in the center.
- Rub the cut sides with lemon halves to prevent discoloration.

2. Grill the Artichokes:
- Preheat the grill to medium-high heat.
- Brush the artichokes with olive oil and season with salt and pepper.
- Grill the artichokes cut side down for about 8-10 minutes or until char marks appear.
- Flip and grill for an additional 5-7 minutes until tender.

3. Prepare the Lemon and Garlic Aioli:
- In a bowl, combine mayonnaise, minced garlic, lemon zest, and lemon juice.
- Season with salt and pepper to taste.
- Mix well and refrigerate until ready to serve.

4. Serve:
- Arrange the grilled artichokes on a platter.
- Serve with a side of Lemon and Garlic Aioli for dipping.

Nutrition Information:

Note: Nutrition values are approximate and may vary based on specific ingredients and serving sizes.

- Calories: 320 per serving
- Total Fat: 24g
- Saturated Fat: 3g
- Trans Fat: 0g
- Cholesterol: 15mg
- Sodium: 400mg
- Total Carbohydrates: 25g
- Dietary Fiber: 10g
- Sugars: 2g
- Protein: 5g

Elevate your dining experience with these Grilled Artichokes, a homage to the culinary excellence found at Nancy Silverton's Mozza restaurant. The smoky essence of the grilled artichokes combined with the zesty Lemon and Garlic Aioli creates a symphony of flavors that will leave your taste buds craving more.

37. Spaghetti with Tomato, Basil, and Parmesan

Indulge your taste buds in the culinary magic inspired by the renowned Nancy Silverton's Mozza restaurant with our delightful recipe for Spaghetti with Tomato, Basil, and Parmesan. This classic Italian dish embodies the essence of Mozza's commitment to fresh, high-quality ingredients and simple, yet bold flavors. Elevate your dining experience at home with this easy-to-follow recipe that captures the essence of Mozza's culinary artistry.

Serving: 4 servings
Preparation Time: 15 minutes
Ready Time: 30 minutes

Ingredients:
- 400g spaghetti
- 2 tbsp olive oil
- 4 garlic cloves, minced
- 800g ripe tomatoes, diced
- 1 tsp red pepper flakes (adjust to taste)
- Salt and black pepper to taste
- 1 cup fresh basil leaves, torn
- 1 cup Parmesan cheese, freshly grated

Instructions:
1. Cook the spaghetti according to the package instructions until al dente. Drain and set aside.
2. In a large skillet, heat olive oil over medium heat. Add minced garlic and sauté until fragrant.
3. Add diced tomatoes to the skillet, stirring occasionally. Allow the tomatoes to cook down and release their juices, creating a rich, flavorful sauce. Season with red pepper flakes, salt, and black pepper to taste.
4. Toss the cooked spaghetti into the tomato sauce, ensuring each strand is generously coated.
5. Remove the skillet from heat and gently fold in torn basil leaves, allowing their fresh aroma to infuse into the dish.
6. Serve the spaghetti in individual plates, topped with a generous sprinkle of freshly grated Parmesan cheese.

Nutrition Information:
(Per Serving)
- Calories: 450

- Protein: 15g
- Carbohydrates: 60g
- Dietary Fiber: 4g
- Sugars: 5g
- Fat: 18g
- Saturated Fat: 6g
- Cholesterol: 20mg
- Sodium: 500mg
- Vitamin D: 2mcg
- Calcium: 250mg
- Iron: 3mg
- Potassium: 700mg

Note: Nutrition information is approximate and may vary based on specific ingredients used. Adjustments can be made according to personal dietary preferences and restrictions. Enjoy this Mozza-inspired masterpiece with friends and family, savoring the flavors that echo the culinary excellence of Nancy Silverton's renowned restaurant.

38. Grilled Calamari with Chickpeas and Salsa Verde

Elevate your culinary experience with this exquisite dish inspired by the renowned flavors of Nancy Silverton's Mozza restaurant. Grilled Calamari with Chickpeas and Salsa Verde combines the freshness of grilled calamari with the heartiness of chickpeas, all brought together with the vibrant flavors of salsa verde. It's a celebration of Mediterranean-inspired ingredients that dance on your palate, creating a symphony of taste and texture.

Serving: 4 servings
Preparation Time: 20 minutes
Ready Time: 30 minutes

Ingredients:
- 1 pound fresh calamari, cleaned and tentacles separated
- 1 can (15 oz) chickpeas, drained and rinsed
- 1/4 cup olive oil
- Salt and pepper to taste

For the Salsa Verde:

- 1 cup fresh parsley, finely chopped
- 1/4 cup fresh mint, finely chopped
- 2 cloves garlic, minced
- 2 tablespoons capers, drained and chopped
- 1 tablespoon Dijon mustard
- 1 tablespoon red wine vinegar
- 1/2 cup extra virgin olive oil
- Salt and pepper to taste

Instructions:

1. Prepare the Salsa Verde:
- In a bowl, combine the chopped parsley, mint, minced garlic, capers, Dijon mustard, and red wine vinegar.
- Slowly whisk in the extra virgin olive oil until the salsa verde reaches a smooth consistency.
- Season with salt and pepper to taste. Set aside.

2. Grill the Calamari:
- Preheat the grill to medium-high heat.
- In a bowl, toss the cleaned calamari and tentacles with olive oil, salt, and pepper.
- Grill the calamari for 2-3 minutes per side or until they have a nice char and are just cooked through.
- Remove from the grill and set aside.

3. Prepare the Chickpeas:
- In a pan over medium heat, warm the chickpeas until heated through.
- Season with salt and pepper to taste.

4. Assemble the Dish:
- On serving plates, arrange a portion of grilled calamari and chickpeas.
- Drizzle the salsa verde generously over the calamari and chickpeas.

5. Serve:
- Garnish with additional fresh herbs if desired.
- Serve immediately and enjoy the burst of Mediterranean flavors.

Nutrition Information:

(Per Serving)
- Calories: 380
- Protein: 22g
- Carbohydrates: 20g
- Fat: 25g
- Fiber: 5g

Delight in the harmonious blend of textures and tastes as Grilled Calamari with Chickpeas and Salsa Verde transports you to the culinary world of Nancy Silverton's Mozza restaurant.

39. Prosciutto and Fig Pizza with Gorgonzola and Balsamic

Indulge your taste buds in a culinary symphony inspired by the renowned Nancy Silverton's Mozza restaurant. This Prosciutto and Fig Pizza with Gorgonzola and Balsamic is a harmonious blend of savory and sweet, capturing the essence of Mozza's delectable menu. Elevate your pizza experience with the richness of prosciutto, the sweetness of figs, the tanginess of gorgonzola, and the depth of balsamic glaze.

Serving: 4 servings
Preparation Time: 20 minutes
Ready Time: 15 minutes

Ingredients:
- 1 pound pizza dough, homemade or store-bought
- 1/2 cup fig jam
- 8 slices prosciutto
- 1 cup crumbled Gorgonzola cheese
- 1/2 cup fresh figs, sliced
- 1/4 cup balsamic glaze
- Fresh arugula for garnish (optional)

Instructions:
1. Preheat your oven to the highest temperature it can reach, typically around 500°F (260°C). If you have a pizza stone, place it in the oven during the preheating process.
2. Roll out the pizza dough on a floured surface to your desired thickness.
3. Spread the fig jam evenly over the pizza dough, leaving a small border around the edges.
4. Lay the prosciutto slices over the fig jam, distributing them evenly across the pizza.
5. Sprinkle the crumbled Gorgonzola cheese over the prosciutto.

6. Arrange the sliced fresh figs on top of the pizza.
7. Carefully transfer the pizza to the preheated pizza stone or a baking sheet if you don't have a stone.
8. Bake in the preheated oven for about 12-15 minutes or until the crust is golden and the toppings are bubbly and slightly browned.
9. Remove the pizza from the oven and drizzle the balsamic glaze over the top.
10. Allow the pizza to cool for a few minutes before slicing. Optionally, garnish with fresh arugula for an extra burst of flavor.

Nutrition Information:
(per serving)
- Calories: 450
- Total Fat: 15g
- Saturated Fat: 7g
- Trans Fat: 0g
- Cholesterol: 30mg
- Sodium: 1100mg
- Total Carbohydrates: 60g
- Dietary Fiber: 3g
- Sugars: 20g
- Protein: 18g

Note: Nutrition information is approximate and may vary based on specific ingredients and portion sizes. Adjust quantities and serving sizes accordingly.

40. Burrata with Roasted Beets, Hazelnuts, and Orange

Indulge in the exquisite flavors of Nancy Silverton's Mozza restaurant with this delectable recipe for Burrata with Roasted Beets, Hazelnuts, and Orange. Inspired by the restaurant's commitment to fresh, high-quality ingredients and inventive combinations, this dish brings together the creaminess of burrata, the earthy sweetness of roasted beets, the crunch of hazelnuts, and the citrusy brightness of orange. Perfect for a sophisticated appetizer or a light and refreshing lunch, this recipe captures the essence of Mozza's culinary artistry.

Serving: 4 servings
Preparation Time: 15 minutes
Ready Time: 45 minutes

Ingredients:
- 8 small beets, mixed colors, peeled and cut into wedges
- 2 tablespoons olive oil
- Salt and pepper to taste
- 1 cup hazelnuts, toasted and roughly chopped
- 1 large burrata cheese ball
- 2 oranges, peeled and segmented
- Zest of 1 orange
- Fresh basil leaves for garnish

Instructions:
1. Roast the Beets:
- Preheat the oven to 400°F (200°C).
- Toss the beet wedges with olive oil, salt, and pepper.
- Spread the beets on a baking sheet in a single layer.
- Roast in the preheated oven for 30-35 minutes or until the beets are tender and caramelized. Allow them to cool slightly.
2. Prepare the Hazelnuts:
- Toast the hazelnuts in a dry skillet over medium heat until fragrant and lightly browned.
- Roughly chop the toasted hazelnuts.
3. Assemble the Dish:
- Place the burrata in the center of a serving platter.
- Arrange the roasted beet wedges around the burrata.
- Sprinkle the chopped hazelnuts over the beets and burrata.
- Scatter orange segments on top.
- Grate the orange zest over the entire dish.
4. Garnish and Serve:
- Garnish with fresh basil leaves for a burst of color and added flavor.
- Serve the burrata dish at room temperature, allowing the flavors to meld.

Nutrition Information:
(Per serving)
- Calories: 350
- Protein: 15g

- Fat: 25g
- Carbohydrates: 20g
- Fiber: 6g
- Sugar: 10g
- Sodium: 300mg

Elevate your dining experience with this Burrata with Roasted Beets, Hazelnuts, and Orange dish—a culinary masterpiece inspired by the renowned Nancy Silverton's Mozza restaurant.

41. Wood-Grilled Pork Chop with Rosemary and Honey

Indulge your senses in the culinary symphony inspired by the iconic menu of Nancy Silverton's Mozza restaurant. Elevate your home cooking with the Wood-Grilled Pork Chop with Rosemary and Honey—a dish that captures the essence of Mozza's commitment to bold flavors and artisanal excellence. The marriage of smoky wood-grilled perfection, fragrant rosemary, and the subtle sweetness of honey will transport you to the heart of Mozza's exquisite dining experience.

Serving: 4 servings
Preparation Time: 15 minutes
Ready Time: 1 hour (including marination and grilling)

Ingredients:
- 4 bone-in pork chops, 1-inch thick
- 1/4 cup olive oil
- 2 tablespoons fresh rosemary, chopped
- 3 cloves garlic, minced
- Salt and black pepper, to taste
- 1/4 cup honey

Instructions:
1. Marination:
- In a bowl, combine olive oil, chopped rosemary, minced garlic, salt, and black pepper.
- Place pork chops in a shallow dish and rub the marinade mixture evenly over each chop.

- Cover the dish and let it marinate in the refrigerator for at least 30 minutes, allowing the flavors to infuse.
2. Preheat the Grill:
- Prepare your grill for direct grilling over medium-high heat.
- If using wood chips, soak them in water for 30 minutes to infuse a smoky flavor.
3. Grilling:
- Remove the pork chops from the refrigerator and let them come to room temperature.
- Brush the grill grates with oil to prevent sticking.
- Place the pork chops on the preheated grill and cook for about 5-7 minutes per side or until the internal temperature reaches 145°F (63°C).
- During the last few minutes of grilling, brush each chop with honey, allowing it to caramelize.
4. Resting:
- Remove the pork chops from the grill and let them rest for 5 minutes before serving. This allows the juices to redistribute, ensuring a juicy and flavorful bite.
5. Serve:
- Plate the wood-grilled pork chops and drizzle any remaining honey over the top.
- Garnish with fresh rosemary sprigs for a visually appealing presentation.

Nutrition Information:
- *Note: Nutritional values may vary based on specific ingredients and portion sizes.*
- Calories: 350 per serving
- Protein: 25g
- Fat: 22g
- Carbohydrates: 14g
- Fiber: 1g
- Sugars: 12g
- Sodium: 600mg

Elevate your home dining experience with this exquisite Wood-Grilled Pork Chop recipe inspired by the culinary magic of Nancy Silverton's Mozza restaurant.

42. Margherita Pizza with Truffle Cheese and Mushrooms

Indulge in the culinary excellence of Nancy Silverton's Mozza restaurant with this delectable Margherita Pizza elevated to new heights. We've added a touch of luxury with truffle cheese and earthy mushrooms, creating a symphony of flavors that will transport you to the heart of Mozza's kitchen. Follow this recipe to recreate a gourmet experience in the comfort of your home.

Serving: 2-4
Preparation Time: 20 minutes
Ready Time: 30 minutes

Ingredients:
- 1 pound pizza dough (store-bought or homemade)
- 1/2 cup pizza sauce
- 1 1/2 cups fresh mozzarella cheese, sliced
- 1/4 cup truffle cheese, shaved or grated
- 1 cup mushrooms, thinly sliced (cremini or wild mushrooms for extra flavor)
- Fresh basil leaves for garnish
- Olive oil for drizzling
- Salt and black pepper to taste
- Flour for dusting

Instructions:
1. Preheat the Oven: Preheat your oven to the highest setting (usually around 475°F/245°C). If you have a pizza stone, place it in the oven to heat as well.
2. Prepare the Dough: Dust a clean surface with flour and roll out the pizza dough to your desired thickness. If you like a thin crust, roll it out more; for a thicker crust, keep it a bit chunkier.
3. Assemble the Pizza: Transfer the rolled-out dough to a pizza peel or an inverted baking sheet dusted with flour. Spread an even layer of pizza sauce over the dough, leaving a small border around the edges.
4. Add the Toppings: Place slices of fresh mozzarella evenly across the pizza. Distribute the sliced mushrooms and sprinkle the truffle cheese on top. Season with salt and black pepper to taste.

5. Bake the Pizza: If using a pizza stone, carefully transfer the pizza onto the preheated stone in the oven. If not using a stone, simply place the baking sheet in the oven. Bake for about 12-15 minutes or until the crust is golden and the cheese is bubbly and slightly browned.
6. Finish and Serve: Remove the pizza from the oven, drizzle with olive oil, and garnish with fresh basil leaves. Allow it to cool for a couple of minutes before slicing.

Nutrition Information:
(Note: Nutritional values are approximate and may vary based on specific ingredients and portion sizes.)
- Calories: 300 per serving
- Total Fat: 12g
- Saturated Fat: 6g
- Cholesterol: 30mg
- Sodium: 600mg
- Total Carbohydrates: 35g
- Dietary Fiber: 2g
- Sugars: 2g
- Protein: 15g

Tip: For an extra burst of flavor, drizzle truffle oil over the pizza just before serving. Enjoy your taste of Mozza's brilliance!

43. Panzanella Salad with Heirloom Tomatoes and Ciabatta

Panzanella Salad with Heirloom Tomatoes and Ciabatta is a vibrant and rustic dish that encapsulates the essence of Nancy Silverton's Mozza restaurant. This salad celebrates the simplicity of Italian cuisine, combining the sweetness of ripe heirloom tomatoes with the crunch of toasted ciabatta, all brought together by a flavorful dressing. It's a refreshing and colorful addition to any meal, perfect for showcasing the freshest ingredients of the season.

Serving: This recipe yields 4 servings.
Preparation time: 15 minutes
Ready time: 30 minutes

Ingredients:
- 4 cups of ripe heirloom tomatoes, assorted colors, sliced into wedges
- 4 cups of day-old ciabatta bread, cut into 1-inch cubes
- 1/2 red onion, thinly sliced
- 1 English cucumber, sliced into half-moons
- 1/2 cup fresh basil leaves, torn
- 1/4 cup capers, drained
- 1/3 cup red wine vinegar
- 1/2 cup extra-virgin olive oil
- Salt and freshly ground black pepper to taste

Instructions:
1. Preheat the oven to 375°F (190°C). Place the ciabatta cubes on a baking sheet and drizzle with a bit of olive oil. Bake for about 10-12 minutes or until the bread turns golden and crispy. Set aside to cool.
2. In a large mixing bowl, combine the sliced tomatoes, red onion, cucumber, torn basil leaves, and capers.
3. In a separate small bowl, whisk together the red wine vinegar, extra-virgin olive oil, salt, and pepper to make the dressing.
4. Add the toasted ciabatta cubes to the bowl with the vegetables.
5. Pour the dressing over the salad and gently toss everything together until the bread soaks up the flavors and the ingredients are well coated.
6. Let the salad sit for about 15-20 minutes before serving, allowing the flavors to meld together.
7. Taste and adjust seasoning if needed before serving. Garnish with additional basil leaves if desired.

Nutrition Information (per serving):
- Calories: 320
- Total Fat: 20g
- Saturated Fat: 3g
- Cholesterol: 0mg
- Sodium: 420mg
- Total Carbohydrate: 30g
- Dietary Fiber: 4g
- Sugars: 7g
- Protein: 5g

Enjoy this Panzanella Salad with Heirloom Tomatoes and Ciabatta as a delightful appetizer or as a light and flavorful main course. The blend of fresh ingredients and zesty dressing makes it a delightful dish that captures the essence of Mozza's menu.

44. Grilled Broccolini with Chili and Garlic

Inspired by the vibrant flavors of Nancy Silverton's renowned Mozza restaurant, this Grilled Broccolini with Chili and Garlic is a delightful marriage of simple ingredients and bold tastes. The smoky char from the grill complements the broccolini's earthy flavor, while the zing from garlic and chili adds a tantalizing kick. Enjoy this dish as a vibrant side or a flavorful standalone dish that embodies the essence of Mozza's culinary prowess.

Serving: 4 servings
Preparation time: 10 minutes
Ready time: 15 minutes

Ingredients:
- 1 bunch broccolini, trimmed
- 3 tablespoons olive oil
- 4 cloves garlic, thinly sliced
- 1 teaspoon red pepper flakes (adjust to taste)
- Salt and pepper to taste
- Lemon wedges (for serving, optional)

Instructions:
1. Preheat a grill or grill pan over medium-high heat.
2. In a bowl, toss the broccolini with 2 tablespoons of olive oil until evenly coated. Season with salt and pepper.
3. Place the broccolini on the grill and cook, turning occasionally, until tender and slightly charred, about 5-7 minutes.
4. While the broccolini is grilling, heat the remaining 1 tablespoon of olive oil in a small pan over medium heat. Add the sliced garlic and red pepper flakes. Cook, stirring frequently, until the garlic turns golden and fragrant, about 1-2 minutes. Be careful not to burn the garlic.
5. Once the broccolini is done, transfer it to a serving platter. Drizzle the garlic and chili mixture over the grilled broccolini.

6. Serve hot, optionally accompanied by lemon wedges for a burst of citrusy flavor.

Nutrition Information (per serving):
- Calories: 110
- Fat: 9g
- Carbohydrates: 6g
- Fiber: 3g
- Protein: 2g

Note: Nutritional values are approximate and may vary based on specific ingredients used. Adjust spice levels according to personal preference.

45. Mozzarella and Tomato Tart with Pesto

Indulge in the culinary elegance inspired by the renowned Nancy Silverton's Mozza restaurant with our delightful Mozzarella and Tomato Tart with Pesto. This recipe captures the essence of Mozza's distinctive flavors, combining the richness of mozzarella, the freshness of tomatoes, and the vibrant kick of homemade pesto. Perfect for any occasion, this tart is a testament to the artistry that defines Mozza's menu.

Serving: Serves 6
Preparation Time: 20 minutes
Ready Time: 45 minutes

Ingredients:
- 1 sheet puff pastry, thawed
- 1 cup fresh mozzarella, sliced
- 2 large tomatoes, thinly sliced
- 1/4 cup pine nuts, toasted
- Fresh basil leaves for garnish

Pesto:
- 2 cups fresh basil leaves, packed
- 1/2 cup grated Parmesan cheese
- 1/2 cup pine nuts
- 2 cloves garlic
- 1/2 cup extra-virgin olive oil
- Salt and pepper to taste

Instructions:
1. Preheat Oven:
Preheat the oven to 400°F (200°C).
2. Prepare Pesto:
a. In a food processor, combine basil, Parmesan, pine nuts, and garlic.
b. Pulse until finely chopped.
c. With the processor running, slowly add olive oil until the mixture is smooth.
d. Season with salt and pepper to taste. Set aside.
3. Roll Out Puff Pastry:
Roll out the puff pastry on a lightly floured surface to fit a tart pan. Press the pastry into the pan and trim any excess.
4. Assemble Tart:
a. Spread a layer of pesto over the puff pastry.
b. Arrange mozzarella slices evenly over the pesto.
c. Place tomato slices on top of the mozzarella.
d. Sprinkle toasted pine nuts over the tomatoes.
5. Bake:
Bake in the preheated oven for 25-30 minutes or until the pastry is golden and the cheese is melted and bubbly.
6. Garnish:
Remove the tart from the oven and let it cool for a few minutes. Garnish with fresh basil leaves.
7. Serve:
Slice and serve the Mozzarella and Tomato Tart warm. Enjoy the harmonious blend of flavors!

Nutrition Information:
Per serving (serves 6):
- Calories: 380
- Total Fat: 28g
- Saturated Fat: 8g
- Trans Fat: 0g
- Cholesterol: 25mg
- Sodium: 380mg
- Total Carbohydrates: 22g
- Dietary Fiber: 2g
- Sugars: 2g
- Protein: 12g

Note: Nutrition information is approximate and may vary based on specific ingredients used.

46. Wood-Grilled Salmon with Lemon and Dill

Experience the exquisite flavors of Nancy Silverton's Mozza restaurant in the comfort of your own home with this Wood-Grilled Salmon with Lemon and Dill recipe. Inspired by the restaurant's commitment to fresh, high-quality ingredients and innovative culinary techniques, this dish promises to elevate your dining experience. The wood-grilling imparts a smoky depth to the succulent salmon, while the vibrant combination of lemon and dill adds a burst of brightness to every bite. Prepare to embark on a culinary journey that captures the essence of Mozza's renowned menu.

Serving: 4 servings
Preparation Time: 15 minutes
Ready Time: 30 minutes

Ingredients:
- 4 salmon fillets, skin-on
- 2 tablespoons olive oil
- Salt and black pepper, to taste
- 2 lemons, thinly sliced
- 4 sprigs fresh dill, chopped
- Wooden skewers, soaked in water for 30 minutes

Instructions:
1. Preheat your wood grill to medium-high heat.
2. Brush the salmon fillets with olive oil and season generously with salt and black pepper.
3. Thread lemon slices onto the soaked wooden skewers, creating a bed for the salmon fillets.
4. Place the salmon fillets on top of the lemon skewers, ensuring they are secure.
5. Carefully place the skewers on the preheated wood grill and cook the salmon for 4-5 minutes per side, or until the fish is opaque and easily flakes with a fork.

6. During the last minute of cooking, sprinkle the chopped dill over the salmon fillets, allowing it to infuse its aromatic flavor.
7. Once done, carefully remove the salmon skewers from the grill.
8. Serve the wood-grilled salmon hot, accompanied by additional lemon wedges and a garnish of fresh dill.

Nutrition Information:
(Per serving)
- Calories: 320
- Total Fat: 18g
- Saturated Fat: 3g
- Trans Fat: 0g
- Cholesterol: 80mg
- Sodium: 90mg
- Total Carbohydrates: 2g
- Dietary Fiber: 1g
- Sugars: 0g
- Protein: 35g

Note: Nutrition values are approximate and may vary based on specific ingredients used. Adjustments can be made based on dietary preferences and restrictions.

47. Burrata with Prosciutto, Melon, and Mint

Indulge your senses with a dish inspired by the exquisite flavors of Nancy Silverton's Mozza restaurant. This Burrata with Prosciutto, Melon, and Mint is a harmonious blend of creamy, savory, and sweet elements that dance on your palate. The rich creaminess of burrata, the saltiness of prosciutto, the juicy sweetness of melon, and the refreshing hint of mint come together to create a dish that exemplifies the culinary artistry of Mozza.

Serving: 4 servings
Preparation Time: 15 minutes
Ready Time: 15 minutes

Ingredients:
- 2 balls of fresh burrata

- 8 slices of prosciutto
- 1 small melon (cantaloupe or honeydew), thinly sliced or balled
- Fresh mint leaves, for garnish
- Extra virgin olive oil, for drizzling
- Balsamic glaze, for drizzling
- Salt and black pepper, to taste

Instructions:

1. Prepare the Ingredients:
- Allow the burrata to come to room temperature for about 15 minutes.
- Arrange the prosciutto slices on a serving platter.
- Slice or ball the melon, and set aside.
2. Assemble the Dish:
- Place the burrata on the center of the prosciutto slices.
3. Enhance with Melon:
- Surround the burrata with the sliced or balled melon.
4. Garnish with Mint:
- Sprinkle fresh mint leaves over the burrata and melon.
5. Season and Drizzle:
- Season the dish with a pinch of salt and black pepper.
- Drizzle extra virgin olive oil and balsamic glaze over the burrata, prosciutto, and melon.
6. Serve:
- Serve immediately to enjoy the contrast of flavors and textures.

Nutrition Information:

(Per Serving)
- Calories: 350
- Protein: 18g
- Fat: 24g
- Carbohydrates: 15g
- Fiber: 2g
- Sugar: 10g
- Sodium: 800mg

Note: Nutrition information is approximate and may vary based on specific ingredients used.

Elevate your dining experience with this Burrata with Prosciutto, Melon, and Mint, a culinary gem inspired by the inventive menu at Nancy Silverton's Mozza restaurant. This dish is not just a feast for the taste buds but also a celebration of vibrant textures and complementary flavors. Enjoy the magic of Mozza in the comfort of your own home.

48. Ricotta and Swiss Chard Cannelloni with Tomato Sauce

Indulge in the culinary brilliance inspired by the famed Mozza restaurant, as we bring you a delectable creation – Ricotta and Swiss Chard Cannelloni with Tomato Sauce. This dish pays homage to the innovative and flavorful menu curated by Nancy Silverton, a culinary icon known for her expertise in crafting dishes that delight the palate. Dive into a world of rich textures and harmonious flavors with this cannelloni that perfectly balances the creamy goodness of ricotta and the earthy notes of Swiss chard, all enveloped in a luscious tomato sauce. Let your taste buds embark on a journey through the essence of Mozza's culinary excellence.

Serving: 4 servings
Preparation Time: 30 minutes
Ready Time: 1 hour 30 minutes

Ingredients:
- 1 box (12 pieces) cannelloni tubes
- 2 cups fresh ricotta cheese
- 1 bunch Swiss chard, finely chopped
- 1 cup grated Parmesan cheese
- 1 egg, beaten
- 2 cloves garlic, minced
- Salt and black pepper to taste
- 2 cups tomato sauce
- 1 cup shredded mozzarella cheese
- Fresh basil leaves for garnish

Instructions:
1. Prepare the Cannelloni Tubes:
- Cook the cannelloni tubes according to the package instructions. Once cooked, drain and set aside to cool.
2. Make the Filling:

- In a mixing bowl, combine ricotta cheese, chopped Swiss chard, Parmesan cheese, minced garlic, beaten egg, salt, and black pepper. Mix until well combined.
3. Fill the Cannelloni Tubes:
- Using a spoon or a piping bag, fill each cannelloni tube with the ricotta and Swiss chard mixture.
4. Assemble the Cannelloni:
- Preheat the oven to 375°F (190°C). Spread a thin layer of tomato sauce on the bottom of a baking dish. Place the filled cannelloni tubes in the dish in a single layer. Pour the remaining tomato sauce over the top and sprinkle with shredded mozzarella.
5. Bake:
- Cover the baking dish with foil and bake in the preheated oven for 30 minutes. Remove the foil and bake for an additional 15-20 minutes or until the cheese is golden and bubbly.
6. Garnish and Serve:
- Remove from the oven and let it rest for a few minutes. Garnish with fresh basil leaves before serving.

Nutrition Information:
Note: Nutrition information is approximate and may vary based on specific ingredients used.
- Calories: 400 per serving
- Protein: 20g
- Fat: 15g
- Carbohydrates: 45g
- Fiber: 5g
- Sugar: 8g
- Sodium: 800mg

Elevate your home cooking with this Mozza-inspired masterpiece, where every bite is a celebration of flavors that echo the culinary genius of Nancy Silverton's renowned restaurant.

49. Margherita Pizza with Black Olives and Anchovies

Indulge in the culinary magic inspired by the iconic Nancy Silverton's Mozza restaurant with our rendition of the classic Margherita Pizza, elevated with the briny goodness of black olives and the savory punch of anchovies. This recipe pays homage to the artisanal approach and exquisite flavors that define Mozza's menu, bringing a taste of the renowned establishment straight to your home.

Serving: Makes one 12-inch pizza, serving 2-4 people.
Preparation Time: 20 minutes
Ready Time: 15-20 minutes

Ingredients:
- 1 pound pizza dough, homemade or store-bought
- 1/2 cup pizza sauce
- 1 1/2 cups fresh mozzarella cheese, sliced
- 1/4 cup Kalamata olives, pitted and sliced
- 2 tablespoons black olives, sliced
- 4-6 anchovy fillets, oil-packed, drained
- Fresh basil leaves, for garnish
- Olive oil, for drizzling
- Flour or cornmeal, for dusting

Instructions:
1. Preheat the Oven:
Preheat your oven to the highest setting (typically around 475-500°F/245-260°C). If you have a pizza stone, place it in the oven during preheating.
2. Prepare the Dough:
On a lightly floured surface, roll out the pizza dough to your desired thickness. If you prefer a thin crust, roll it out more; for a thicker crust, keep it a bit thicker.
3. Assemble the Pizza:
Place the rolled-out dough on a pizza peel or parchment paper. Spread the pizza sauce evenly over the dough, leaving a small border for the crust. Arrange the fresh mozzarella slices on top.
4. Add Toppings:
Sprinkle the Kalamata olives and black olives over the pizza. Distribute the anchovy fillets evenly across the pizza. If desired, add more fresh mozzarella on top.
5. Bake the Pizza:
If using a pizza stone, carefully transfer the pizza (with parchment paper) onto the preheated stone in the oven. If not using a stone, place the

pizza directly on a baking sheet. Bake for 15-20 minutes or until the crust is golden and the cheese is bubbly and slightly browned.
6. Finish and Serve:
Once out of the oven, drizzle the pizza with olive oil and garnish with fresh basil leaves. Allow it to cool for a few minutes before slicing. Serve hot and enjoy the flavors reminiscent of Mozza's culinary excellence.

Nutrition Information:
(Per serving, based on 4 servings)
- Calories: 450
- Total Fat: 18g
- Saturated Fat: 8g
- Trans Fat: 0g
- Cholesterol: 35mg
- Sodium: 1200mg
- Total Carbohydrates: 50g
- Dietary Fiber: 3g
- Sugars: 3g
- Protein: 20g
Note: Nutrition information is approximate and may vary based on specific ingredients used.

50. Wood-Roasted Chicken with Lemon and Herbs

Indulge in the rustic charm of Nancy Silverton's Mozza restaurant with this exquisite Wood-Roasted Chicken with Lemon and Herbs recipe. Inspired by the bold flavors and expert craftsmanship of Mozza's menu, this dish is a testament to the artistry of wood-fired cooking. The succulent chicken, infused with the essence of lemon and aromatic herbs, promises a symphony of flavors that will transport your taste buds straight to the heart of Mozza's culinary magic.

Serving: Serves 4
Preparation Time: 15 minutes
Ready Time: 1 hour 30 minutes

Ingredients:
- 1 whole chicken (approximately 3-4 pounds)

- 2 lemons, thinly sliced
- 4 cloves garlic, minced
- 2 tablespoons fresh rosemary, finely chopped
- 2 tablespoons fresh thyme, leaves only
- Salt and pepper to taste
- 1/4 cup olive oil
- Wood chips for smoking (preferably fruitwood like apple or cherry)

Instructions:

1. Preheat the Wood-Fired Oven or Grill:

- If using a wood-fired oven or grill, preheat it to around 375°F (190°C). Ensure that the wood chips are ready for smoking.

2. Prepare the Chicken:

- Rinse the whole chicken under cold water and pat it dry with paper towels.
- Season the chicken generously with salt and pepper, both inside and out.

3. Create Herb and Lemon Mixture:

- In a small bowl, combine minced garlic, chopped rosemary, thyme leaves, and olive oil.
- Toss in the lemon slices and coat them with the herb mixture.

4. Infuse the Chicken:

- Gently lift the chicken's skin and rub the herb and lemon mixture underneath, ensuring even distribution.
- Place a few lemon slices inside the cavity of the chicken for added flavor.

5. Truss the Chicken:

- Truss the chicken using kitchen twine to maintain its shape during cooking.

6. Wood-Roasting:

- Place the seasoned chicken on a roasting pan or directly on the grill grates.
- If using wood chips for smoking, scatter them over the hot coals or in the wood box of your grill.
- Roast the chicken for about 1 hour and 15 minutes or until the internal temperature reaches 165°F (74°C), basting with the pan juices every 20-30 minutes.

7. Rest and Serve:

- Allow the chicken to rest for 10-15 minutes before carving.

- Serve the wood-roasted chicken with the remaining lemon and herb mixture as a garnish.

Nutrition Information:
(Per serving)
- Calories: 400
- Protein: 25g
- Carbohydrates: 5g
- Fat: 32g
- Saturated Fat: 7g
- Cholesterol: 95mg
- Sodium: 500mg
- Fiber: 2g
- Sugar: 1g

Elevate your home-cooking experience with the Mozza-inspired Wood-Roasted Chicken, a culinary journey that captures the essence of Nancy Silverton's acclaimed restaurant.

51. Grilled Romaine Salad with Caesar Dressing and Croutons

Indulge in the culinary excellence inspired by Nancy Silverton's iconic Mozza restaurant with our Grilled Romaine Salad featuring the classic Caesar dressing and homemade croutons. This sophisticated twist on the traditional Caesar salad elevates the flavors with the smoky essence of grilled romaine lettuce, creating a dish that embodies the essence of Mozza's renowned menu.

Serving: 4 servings
Preparation Time: 15 minutes
Ready Time: 25 minutes

Ingredients:
For the Caesar Dressing:
- 1/2 cup mayonnaise
- 2 tablespoons Dijon mustard
- 2 tablespoons grated Parmesan cheese
- 1 tablespoon red wine vinegar

- 1 teaspoon Worcestershire sauce
- 2 cloves garlic, minced
- Salt and pepper to taste

For the Croutons:
- 4 cups cubed rustic bread
- 2 tablespoons olive oil
- 1 teaspoon garlic powder
- Salt and pepper to taste

For the Grilled Romaine:
- 2 large heads of romaine lettuce, halved lengthwise
- Olive oil for brushing
- Salt and pepper to taste

Optional Toppings:
- Shaved Parmesan cheese
- Cherry tomatoes, halved

Instructions:

1. Prepare the Caesar Dressing:
- In a bowl, whisk together mayonnaise, Dijon mustard, Parmesan cheese, red wine vinegar, Worcestershire sauce, minced garlic, salt, and pepper. Set aside.

2. Make the Croutons:
- Preheat the oven to 375°F (190°C).
- Toss the cubed bread with olive oil, garlic powder, salt, and pepper.
- Spread the seasoned bread on a baking sheet and bake for 10-12 minutes or until golden brown. Set aside.

3. Grill the Romaine:
- Preheat a grill or grill pan over medium-high heat.
- Brush the cut sides of the romaine lettuce with olive oil and sprinkle with salt and pepper.
- Grill the romaine for 2-3 minutes per side or until lightly charred.

4. Assemble the Salad:
- Place the grilled romaine on serving plates.
- Drizzle the Caesar dressing over the lettuce.
- Sprinkle with homemade croutons and optional toppings like shaved Parmesan and cherry tomatoes.

5. Serve:
- Serve immediately and enjoy the perfect harmony of smoky, grilled goodness and the rich flavors of Caesar dressing.

Nutrition Information:
(Per serving)
- Calories: 350
- Total Fat: 25g
- Saturated Fat: 5g
- Trans Fat: 0g
- Cholesterol: 20mg
- Sodium: 550mg
- Total Carbohydrates: 25g
- Dietary Fiber: 3g
- Sugars: 3g
- Protein: 8g

Savor the exquisite taste of Mozza in the comfort of your home with this Grilled Romaine Salad, a delightful addition to your culinary repertoire.

52. Prosciutto and Burrata Pizza with Arugula

Indulge in the exquisite flavors reminiscent of Nancy Silverton's Mozza restaurant with our Prosciutto and Burrata Pizza with Arugula. This culinary masterpiece combines the richness of creamy burrata, the savory allure of prosciutto, and the peppery kick of arugula on a perfectly baked pizza crust. Inspired by the renowned dishes at Mozza, this pizza promises a symphony of textures and tastes that will transport your taste buds to the heart of Italian gastronomy.

Serving: Serves 4
Preparation Time: 20 minutes
Ready Time: 15 minutes

Ingredients:
- 1 pound pizza dough, at room temperature
- 1/4 cup extra-virgin olive oil
- 1 clove garlic, minced
- 8 ounces fresh burrata cheese, torn into small pieces
- 4 ounces thinly sliced prosciutto
- 2 cups arugula, washed and dried
- 1/2 cup freshly grated Parmesan cheese
- Salt and black pepper to taste

- Red pepper flakes (optional, for extra heat)

Instructions:

1. Preheat the Oven:
Preheat your oven to 475°F (245°C). If you have a pizza stone, place it in the oven during preheating to ensure it gets nice and hot.
2. Prepare the Dough:
On a floured surface, roll out the pizza dough to your desired thickness. If you prefer a thin crust, roll it out thinly; for a thicker crust, leave it a bit thicker.
3. Create the Garlic Oil:
In a small bowl, mix the minced garlic with the extra-virgin olive oil. Brush the garlic oil evenly over the rolled-out pizza dough, leaving a small border around the edges.
4. Assemble the Pizza:
Distribute the torn burrata evenly over the oiled dough. Arrange the prosciutto slices on top of the burrata. Sprinkle Parmesan cheese over the pizza, and season with salt and black pepper to taste.
5. Bake:
If you're using a pizza stone, carefully transfer the assembled pizza onto the hot stone in the oven. Bake for about 12-15 minutes, or until the crust is golden and the cheese is melted and bubbly.
6. Add the Arugula:
Once out of the oven, scatter the fresh arugula over the hot pizza. The residual heat will slightly wilt the arugula. If desired, sprinkle red pepper flakes for an extra kick.
7. Slice and Serve:
Allow the pizza to cool for a few minutes before slicing. Serve slices of this Prosciutto and Burrata Pizza with Arugula as a delectable homage to the flavors of Mozza.

Nutrition Information:

(Per serving)

- Calories: 480
- Fat: 28g
- Saturated Fat: 10g
- Cholesterol: 50mg
- Sodium: 1100mg
- Carbohydrates: 40g
- Fiber: 2g

- Sugar: 1g
- Protein: 18g

Note: Nutritional values are approximate and may vary based on specific ingredients used.

53. Wood-Grilled Bratwurst with Sauerkraut and Mustard

Indulge in the savory delights inspired by the culinary genius of Nancy Silverton's Mozza restaurant with our Wood-Grilled Bratwurst with Sauerkraut and Mustard. This recipe captures the essence of Mozza's commitment to quality and flavor, bringing you a symphony of tastes that will transport you straight to the heart of exceptional dining. The wood-grilled bratwurst, paired with tangy sauerkraut and zesty mustard, creates a harmonious blend that's both comforting and exciting. Elevate your home cooking experience with this delectable dish that mirrors the excellence of Mozza's renowned menu.

Serving: 4 servings
Preparation Time: 15 minutes
Ready Time: 35 minutes

Ingredients:
- 4 bratwurst sausages
- 2 cups sauerkraut, drained
- 1 tablespoon olive oil
- Salt and pepper to taste
- 1/2 cup Dijon mustard
- 4 crusty rolls for serving

Instructions:
1. Preheat your wood-grill to medium-high heat.
2. In a skillet over medium heat, add olive oil. Once hot, add sauerkraut and sauté for 3-5 minutes or until warmed through. Season with salt and pepper to taste. Set aside.
3. Grill the bratwurst sausages on the wood-grill, turning occasionally, until they are evenly browned and cooked through. This should take about 15-20 minutes.

4. While the bratwurst is grilling, split the rolls and warm them on the grill for a couple of minutes until they develop a light toasty crust.
5. Assemble the dish by placing a grilled bratwurst in each roll. Top with a generous portion of sauerkraut and a dollop of Dijon mustard.
6. Serve the Wood-Grilled Bratwurst with Sauerkraut and Mustard hot off the grill. Pair it with your favorite side dishes or enjoy it on its own for a taste reminiscent of Mozza's culinary excellence.

Nutrition Information:
(Per serving)
- Calories: 450
- Total Fat: 25g
- Saturated Fat: 8g
- Cholesterol: 60mg
- Sodium: 1200mg
- Total Carbohydrates: 38g
- Dietary Fiber: 3g
- Sugars: 5g
- Protein: 18g

Note: Nutrition information is approximate and may vary based on specific ingredients and portion sizes used. Adjust quantities to meet your dietary preferences and needs.

54. Eggplant Parmesan with Tomato Sauce and Mozzarella

Indulge in the culinary artistry inspired by Nancy Silverton's renowned Mozza restaurant with our rendition of Eggplant Parmesan with Tomato Sauce and Mozzarella. This classic Italian dish takes on a Mozza twist, marrying the rich flavors of roasted eggplant, velvety tomato sauce, and gooey mozzarella. Elevate your dining experience with this delectable homage to the iconic restaurant.

Serving: 4 servings
Preparation Time: 15 minutes
Ready Time: 1 hour 15 minutes

Ingredients:

- 2 large eggplants, sliced into 1/2-inch rounds
- 1 cup all-purpose flour
- 3 large eggs, beaten
- 2 cups breadcrumbs
- 1 cup freshly grated Parmesan cheese
- Salt and pepper to taste
- 2 cups marinara sauce (homemade or store-bought)
- 2 cups shredded mozzarella cheese
- Fresh basil leaves for garnish

Instructions:

1. Prepare the Eggplant:
- Preheat your oven to 375°F (190°C).
- Sprinkle the eggplant slices with salt and let them sit for 15 minutes to draw out excess moisture.
- Pat the eggplant slices dry with a paper towel.
- Dredge each slice in flour, dip in beaten eggs, and coat with a mixture of breadcrumbs and Parmesan cheese.
2. Bake the Eggplant:
- Place the coated eggplant slices on a baking sheet lined with parchment paper.
- Bake for 25-30 minutes or until the eggplant is golden brown and crispy.
3. Layering:
- In a baking dish, spread a thin layer of marinara sauce.
- Arrange a layer of baked eggplant slices over the sauce.
- Sprinkle mozzarella cheese on top.
- Repeat the layers, finishing with a generous layer of mozzarella on top.
4. Bake to Perfection:
- Bake in the preheated oven for an additional 30-35 minutes or until the cheese is melted and bubbly, and the edges are golden brown.
5. Garnish and Serve:
- Remove from the oven and let it rest for a few minutes.
- Garnish with fresh basil leaves before serving.

Nutrition Information:

(per serving)
- Calories: 450
- Total Fat: 20g
- Saturated Fat: 10g

- Cholesterol: 120mg
- Sodium: 900mg
- Total Carbohydrates: 45g
- Dietary Fiber: 8g
- Sugars: 10g
- Protein: 25g

Indulge in the symphony of flavors that Mozza restaurant has inspired, as you savor the textures and tastes of this Eggplant Parmesan with Tomato Sauce and Mozzarella. Each bite is a celebration of culinary excellence, a testament to the influence of Nancy Silverton's iconic establishment.

55. Margherita Pizza with Gorgonzola and Walnuts

Indulge your taste buds in a symphony of flavors with this delectable Margherita Pizza with Gorgonzola and Walnuts—a culinary masterpiece inspired by the renowned menu of Nancy Silverton's Mozza restaurant. This pizza combines the classic simplicity of a Margherita with the bold richness of Gorgonzola and the satisfying crunch of toasted walnuts. Elevate your pizza game with this unique and mouthwatering creation that pays homage to the culinary brilliance of Mozza.

Serving: Makes 1 pizza (approximately 8 slices)
Preparation Time: 15 minutes
Ready Time: 20 minutes

Ingredients:
- 1 pizza dough ball (store-bought or homemade)
- 1/2 cup pizza sauce
- 1 1/2 cups fresh mozzarella, sliced
- 1/4 cup Gorgonzola cheese, crumbled
- 1/3 cup walnuts, toasted and roughly chopped
- Fresh basil leaves, for garnish
- Olive oil, for drizzling
- Salt and pepper, to taste

Instructions:
1. Preheat the Oven:

Preheat your oven to the highest temperature it can reach, typically around 475°F (245°C).

2. Prepare the Pizza Dough:

Roll out the pizza dough on a floured surface to your desired thickness. If you prefer a thin crust, roll it out thinner.

3. Assemble the Pizza:

Spread the pizza sauce evenly over the rolled-out dough, leaving a small border around the edges. Arrange the fresh mozzarella slices on top, followed by crumbled Gorgonzola and toasted walnuts.

4. Bake to Perfection:

Place the assembled pizza on a preheated pizza stone or baking sheet. Bake in the preheated oven until the crust is golden and the cheese is melted and bubbly, about 12-15 minutes.

5. Finish and Garnish:

Remove the pizza from the oven and let it cool slightly. Drizzle with olive oil, sprinkle with salt and pepper to taste, and garnish with fresh basil leaves.

6. Slice and Serve:

Slice the pizza into wedges and serve immediately, savoring the perfect combination of gooey mozzarella, pungent Gorgonzola, and the satisfying crunch of walnuts.

Nutrition Information:

Note: Nutrition information is approximate and may vary based on specific ingredients and serving sizes.

- Calories per slice: ~250
- Total Fat: ~12g
- Saturated Fat: ~5g
- Trans Fat: 0g
- Cholesterol: ~20mg
- Sodium: ~500mg
- Total Carbohydrates: ~25g
- Dietary Fiber: ~2g
- Sugars: ~2g
- Protein: ~10g

Savor the culinary magic of Mozza with this Margherita Pizza, where traditional meets inventive for a pizza experience like no other!

56. Shrimp and Calamari Salad with White Beans and Lemon

Indulge in the vibrant and refreshing flavors of Nancy Silverton's Mozza restaurant with our delightful Shrimp and Calamari Salad with White Beans and Lemon. This exquisite dish combines succulent seafood with wholesome white beans, all dressed in a zesty lemon vinaigrette. The perfect blend of textures and tastes makes this salad a standout choice, capturing the essence of Mozza's culinary excellence. Prepare to embark on a culinary journey that pays homage to the renowned restaurant's commitment to quality and innovation.

Serving: 4 servings
Preparation Time: 20 minutes
Ready Time: 30 minutes

Ingredients:
- 1/2 pound large shrimp, peeled and deveined
- 1/2 pound calamari rings
- 1 can (15 ounces) white beans, drained and rinsed
- 1 cup cherry tomatoes, halved
- 1/2 cup red onion, finely diced
- 1/4 cup fresh parsley, chopped
- 1/4 cup extra-virgin olive oil
- 2 tablespoons fresh lemon juice
- 1 teaspoon lemon zest
- Salt and pepper to taste
- Mixed salad greens for serving

Instructions:
1. In a large pot of salted boiling water, blanch the shrimp and calamari for 1-2 minutes until they turn opaque. Immediately transfer them to an ice bath to cool. Drain and set aside.
2. In a large bowl, combine the blanched shrimp and calamari with white beans, cherry tomatoes, red onion, and fresh parsley.
3. In a small bowl, whisk together the olive oil, lemon juice, lemon zest, salt, and pepper to create the vinaigrette.
4. Pour the lemon vinaigrette over the seafood and bean mixture. Gently toss to coat all ingredients evenly.

5. To serve, arrange a bed of mixed salad greens on each plate and top with the shrimp and calamari salad.
6. Garnish with additional parsley and lemon slices if desired. Serve immediately and enjoy the burst of Mediterranean flavors.

Nutrition Information:
(Per Serving)
- Calories: 320
- Protein: 22g
- Carbohydrates: 20g
- Fiber: 5g
- Sugars: 2g
- Fat: 18g
- Saturated Fat: 2.5g
- Cholesterol: 120mg
- Sodium: 480mg
Note: Nutrition information is approximate and may vary based on specific ingredients used.

57. Burrata with Heirloom Tomatoes and Balsamic Reduction

Indulge in the sumptuous flavors reminiscent of Nancy Silverton's iconic Mozza restaurant with this exquisite recipe for Burrata with Heirloom Tomatoes and Balsamic Reduction. A celebration of freshness and simplicity, this dish captures the essence of Mozza's commitment to quality ingredients and vibrant taste profiles. Perfect for a light summer appetizer or a sophisticated addition to any gathering, this dish is a testament to the culinary excellence that defines Mozza's menu.

Serving: Ideal as an appetizer, this recipe serves 4.
Preparation Time: 15 minutes
Ready Time: 15 minutes

Ingredients:
- 4 balls of fresh burrata cheese
- 2 cups heirloom tomatoes, assorted colors, sliced
- 1/4 cup fresh basil leaves, torn

- 1/4 cup extra-virgin olive oil
- Salt and pepper to taste
- Balsamic reduction (store-bought or homemade)

Instructions:
1. Prepare Burrata: Place each burrata ball on a serving plate, allowing them to come to room temperature for the fullest flavor.
2. Arrange Tomatoes: Artfully arrange the sliced heirloom tomatoes around the burrata, creating a visually appealing display of colors.
3. Drizzle with Olive Oil: Generously drizzle extra-virgin olive oil over the burrata and tomatoes. This step adds richness and enhances the creamy texture of the burrata.
4. Season: Sprinkle salt and pepper to taste over the tomatoes and burrata. The seasoning will bring out the natural flavors of the ingredients.
5. Garnish with Basil: Scatter torn fresh basil leaves over the dish, adding a fragrant and herbaceous note that complements the creamy burrata and sweet tomatoes.
6. Balsamic Elegance: Finish the dish by delicately drizzling balsamic reduction over the burrata and tomatoes. The sweet and tangy reduction adds a touch of sophistication to the ensemble.
7. Serve: Present immediately to enjoy the dish at its freshest. Serve with crusty bread or crostini to savor every bit of the creamy burrata and juicy heirloom tomatoes.

Nutrition Information:
(Per Serving)
- Calories: 350
- Protein: 12g
- Fat: 30g
- Carbohydrates: 10g
- Fiber: 2g
- Sugar: 5g
- Sodium: 450mg

Elevate your dining experience with this Burrata with Heirloom Tomatoes and Balsamic Reduction, inspired by the culinary finesse of Nancy Silverton's Mozza restaurant. Delight in the harmonious blend of textures and flavors that make this dish a standout on any table.

58. Grilled Lamb Sausage with Mint Pesto and Yogurt

Indulge in the tantalizing flavors inspired by Nancy Silverton's renowned Mozza restaurant with our Grilled Lamb Sausage with Mint Pesto and Yogurt. This dish pays homage to the vibrant and eclectic menu that has made Mozza a culinary destination. The succulent lamb sausage, infused with aromatic spices, is complemented by the freshness of mint pesto and the creaminess of yogurt, creating a symphony of tastes that will transport you to the heart of Mozza's kitchen.

Serving: 4 servings
Preparation Time: 15 minutes
Ready Time: 30 minutes

Ingredients:
- 1 pound lamb sausages
- 1 cup fresh mint leaves, tightly packed
- 1/2 cup pine nuts, toasted
- 2 cloves garlic, peeled
- 1/2 cup grated Pecorino Romano cheese
- 1/2 cup extra-virgin olive oil, divided
- Salt and pepper to taste
- 1 cup Greek yogurt

Instructions:
1. Prepare the Mint Pesto:
- In a food processor, combine the mint leaves, toasted pine nuts, garlic, and Pecorino Romano cheese.
- Pulse the ingredients until coarsely chopped.
- With the food processor running, gradually add 1/4 cup of olive oil until the pesto reaches a smooth consistency.
- Season with salt and pepper to taste.
2. Grill the Lamb Sausages:
- Preheat the grill to medium-high heat.
- Grill the lamb sausages for 8-10 minutes, turning occasionally, until they are cooked through and have a beautiful char on the outside.
3. Prepare Yogurt Sauce:
- In a small bowl, mix the Greek yogurt with a pinch of salt.

4. Assemble:
- Place the grilled lamb sausages on a serving platter.
- Drizzle the mint pesto over the sausages, and serve with a dollop of the yogurt sauce on the side.
5. Garnish:
- Optionally, garnish with additional fresh mint leaves and a sprinkle of pine nuts for added texture and visual appeal.

Nutrition Information:
Note: Nutritional values are approximate and may vary based on specific ingredients used.
- Calories: 450 per serving
- Protein: 18g
- Fat: 38g
- Carbohydrates: 5g
- Fiber: 2g
- Sugar: 1g
- Sodium: 700mg

Indulge in the flavors of Mozza with this Grilled Lamb Sausage dish, marrying the richness of lamb, the vibrancy of mint pesto, and the coolness of yogurt. Perfect for a cozy dinner or a festive gathering, this recipe captures the essence of the culinary magic that defines Nancy Silverton's iconic restaurant.

59. Wood-Grilled Halibut with Roasted Tomatoes and Capers

Indulge in the tantalizing flavors of Nancy Silverton's Mozza restaurant with this exquisite recipe for Wood-Grilled Halibut with Roasted Tomatoes and Capers. Inspired by the culinary finesse of Mozza, this dish captures the essence of fresh, high-quality ingredients combined to create a symphony of taste. The wood-grilled halibut is perfectly complemented by the sweetness of roasted tomatoes and the briny kick of capers, resulting in a dish that exemplifies the restaurant's commitment to culinary excellence.

Serving: 4 servings
Preparation Time: 15 minutes

Ready Time: 30 minutes

Ingredients:
- 4 halibut fillets (6 ounces each)
- 2 cups cherry tomatoes, halved
- 2 tablespoons capers, drained
- 2 tablespoons fresh parsley, chopped
- 2 tablespoons extra-virgin olive oil
- 1 tablespoon balsamic vinegar
- 1 teaspoon lemon zest
- 1 teaspoon salt
- 1/2 teaspoon black pepper
- Wooden skewers, soaked in water

Instructions:
1. Preheat the Grill:
- Preheat a wood-fired grill to medium-high heat. The natural smokiness of the wood will enhance the flavor of the halibut.
2. Prepare the Skewers:
- Thread the halved cherry tomatoes onto the soaked wooden skewers, alternating with capers. This will make them easier to grill and add a delightful presentation to the dish.
3. Season the Halibut:
- Rub the halibut fillets with olive oil, balsamic vinegar, lemon zest, salt, and black pepper, ensuring each fillet is evenly coated with the flavorful mixture.
4. Grill the Halibut:
- Place the seasoned halibut fillets directly on the preheated grill. Grill for about 4-5 minutes per side or until the fish is opaque and easily flakes with a fork.
5. Grill the Tomato Skewers:
- Place the tomato and caper skewers on the grill, turning occasionally, until the tomatoes are slightly charred and softened.
6. Assemble the Dish:
- Arrange the grilled halibut fillets on a serving platter. Top them with the wood-grilled tomato and caper skewers. Sprinkle with fresh chopped parsley.
7. Serve:

- Drizzle with additional olive oil and balsamic vinegar if desired. Serve immediately, and enjoy the vibrant flavors reminiscent of Mozza's exceptional menu.

Nutrition Information:
(Per serving)
- Calories: 320
- Protein: 38g
- Carbohydrates: 6g
- Fat: 16g
- Saturated Fat: 2.5g
- Cholesterol: 75mg
- Sodium: 800mg
- Fiber: 2g
- Sugar: 3g

Elevate your home cooking experience with this Mozza-inspired dish that brings the sophistication of Nancy Silverton's renowned restaurant to your table.

60. Farro Salad with Roasted Vegetables and Feta

Experience the exquisite flavors of Mozza restaurant brought to your own kitchen with this delightful Farro Salad. Inspired by the culinary genius of Nancy Silverton, this dish combines the nutty taste of farro with the earthy goodness of roasted vegetables, all brought together by the rich tang of feta. A wholesome and satisfying dish that captures the essence of Mozza's culinary excellence.

Serving: 4 servings
Preparation Time: 15 minutes
Ready Time: 45 minutes

Ingredients:
- 1 cup farro, rinsed
- 2 cups mixed vegetables (zucchini, cherry tomatoes, bell peppers), diced
- 2 tablespoons olive oil
- Salt and pepper to taste
- 1/2 cup crumbled feta cheese

- 1/4 cup fresh basil leaves, torn

Instructions:

1. Preheat and Roast:
- Preheat your oven to 400°F (200°C).
- In a baking sheet, toss the diced vegetables with olive oil, salt, and pepper.
- Roast the vegetables in the preheated oven for about 25-30 minutes or until they are golden brown and tender.
2. Cook Farro:
- While the vegetables are roasting, cook the farro according to the package instructions. Usually, it takes about 15-20 minutes. Once cooked, drain any excess water.
3. Combine:
- In a large mixing bowl, combine the cooked farro and roasted vegetables.
4. Add Feta and Basil:
- Gently fold in the crumbled feta cheese and torn basil leaves into the farro and vegetable mixture.
5. Adjust Seasoning:
- Taste and adjust the seasoning with salt and pepper as needed.
6. Serve:
- Serve the farro salad at room temperature or slightly chilled.

Nutrition Information:

- *Serving Size:* 1/4 of the recipe
- *Calories:* Approximately 320
- *Total Fat:* 14g
- *Saturated Fat:* 4g
- *Cholesterol:* 15mg
- *Sodium:* 330mg
- *Total Carbohydrates:* 42g
- *Dietary Fiber:* 8g
- *Sugars:* 3g
- *Protein:* 10g

Note: Nutrition information is approximate and may vary based on specific ingredients and portion sizes used. Adjustments can be made to suit dietary preferences and restrictions. Enjoy your delicious Farro Salad with Roasted Vegetables and Feta inspired by the renowned flavors of Nancy Silverton's Mozza restaurant!

61. Margherita Pizza with Pesto and Pine Nuts

Indulge your taste buds in a symphony of flavors with our rendition of Nancy Silverton's Mozza restaurant's signature Margherita Pizza with Pesto and Pine Nuts. This culinary masterpiece marries the classic simplicity of a Margherita pizza with the vibrant kick of pesto and the rich crunch of pine nuts. Each bite is a journey through the renowned flavors that make Mozza a gastronomic haven. Prepare to elevate your pizza game to new heights!

Serving: Makes one 12-inch pizza, serving 2-3 people.
Preparation Time: 20 minutes
Ready Time: 15 minutes (plus dough rising time, if homemade)

Ingredients:
- 1 pizza dough (store-bought or homemade)
- 1/2 cup marinara sauce
- 8 oz fresh mozzarella cheese, thinly sliced
- 1/4 cup grated Parmesan cheese
- 1/4 cup pine nuts, toasted
- Fresh basil leaves for garnish

For the Pesto:
- 2 cups fresh basil leaves, packed
- 1/2 cup grated Parmesan cheese
- 1/2 cup pine nuts
- 2 garlic cloves
- 1/2 cup extra-virgin olive oil
- Salt and pepper to taste

Instructions:
1. Preheat the Oven:
Preheat your oven to the highest setting (usually around 475°F/245°C). If you have a pizza stone, place it in the oven to heat.
2. Prepare the Pesto:
a. In a food processor, combine basil, Parmesan, pine nuts, and garlic.
b. Pulse until coarsely chopped.

c. With the processor running, slowly pour in the olive oil until the pesto reaches a smooth consistency.
d. Season with salt and pepper to taste. Set aside.
3. Roll Out the Dough:
Roll out the pizza dough on a lightly floured surface to your desired thickness.
4. Assemble the Pizza:
a. Transfer the rolled-out dough to a pizza peel or an inverted baking sheet dusted with flour or cornmeal.
b. Spread marinara sauce evenly over the dough, leaving a small border for the crust.
c. Arrange the fresh mozzarella slices on top.
d. Drizzle pesto over the pizza and sprinkle with grated Parmesan.
5. Bake the Pizza:
a. If using a pizza stone, carefully transfer the pizza onto the preheated stone in the oven.
b. Bake for about 12-15 minutes or until the crust is golden and the cheese is bubbly and slightly browned.
6. Toast the Pine Nuts:
While the pizza is baking, toast the pine nuts in a dry skillet over medium heat until golden brown and fragrant.
7. Finish and Serve:
a. Once out of the oven, sprinkle the toasted pine nuts over the hot pizza.
b. Garnish with fresh basil leaves.
c. Slice and serve immediately.

Nutrition Information:
(Per serving, based on 3 servings)
- Calories: 600
- Protein: 20g
- Carbohydrates: 40g
- Fat: 45g
- Saturated Fat: 12g
- Cholesterol: 40mg
- Fiber: 4g
- Sugars: 2g
- Sodium: 800mg

Indulge in the culinary delight of this Margherita Pizza with Pesto and Pine Nuts – a tantalizing fusion of Mozza-inspired brilliance!

62. Fried Green Tomatoes with Burrata and Basil

Indulge in the tantalizing flavors inspired by Nancy Silverton's renowned Mozza restaurant with our delectable recipe for Fried Green Tomatoes with Burrata and Basil. This dish captures the essence of Mozza's menu, offering a perfect balance of crispiness, creaminess, and freshness. The vibrant green tomatoes, golden-fried to perfection, are paired with creamy burrata and aromatic basil, creating a symphony of flavors that will transport you to the heart of culinary excellence.

Serving: 4 servings
Preparation Time: 15 minutes
Ready Time: 25 minutes

Ingredients:
- 4 large green tomatoes, sliced into 1/2-inch rounds
- 1 cup buttermilk
- 1 cup all-purpose flour
- 1 cup cornmeal
- 1 teaspoon smoked paprika
- 1 teaspoon garlic powder
- Salt and pepper to taste
- Vegetable oil for frying
- 1 pound burrata cheese
- Fresh basil leaves for garnish

Instructions:
1. Prep the Tomatoes:
- Place the green tomato slices in a shallow dish and pour the buttermilk over them. Allow them to soak for at least 10 minutes, ensuring each slice is well-coated.
2. Prepare the Coating:
- In a separate bowl, combine the flour, cornmeal, smoked paprika, garlic powder, salt, and pepper. Mix well to create the coating mixture.
3. Coat the Tomatoes:

- Heat vegetable oil in a large skillet over medium-high heat. Take each buttermilk-soaked tomato slice, dredge it in the coating mixture, ensuring an even and generous coating on both sides.
4. Fry the Tomatoes:
- Carefully place the coated tomato slices into the hot oil and fry until golden brown on each side, approximately 2-3 minutes per side. Once fried, transfer them to a paper towel-lined plate to absorb any excess oil.
5. Assemble the Dish:
- Arrange the fried green tomatoes on a serving platter. Tear the burrata into bite-sized pieces and scatter them over the tomatoes.
6. Garnish:
- Garnish the dish with fresh basil leaves, adding a burst of color and aromatic freshness.
7. Serve:
- Serve the Fried Green Tomatoes with Burrata and Basil immediately, allowing the creamy burrata to melt slightly over the warm, crispy tomatoes.

Nutrition Information:
(Per Serving)
- Calories: 480
- Total Fat: 28g
- Saturated Fat: 15g
- Trans Fat: 0g
- Cholesterol: 80mg
- Sodium: 580mg
- Total Carbohydrates: 38g
- Dietary Fiber: 4g
- Sugars: 6g
- Protein: 18g

Indulge in this exquisite dish that pays homage to the culinary genius of Nancy Silverton's Mozza restaurant, where each bite is a celebration of flavor and texture.

63. Wood-Grilled Quail with Pancetta and Balsamic Glaze

Indulge in the rustic charm and robust flavors of Nancy Silverton's Mozza restaurant with our Wood-Grilled Quail featuring the perfect balance of smokiness, richness, and a touch of sweetness. This recipe captures the essence of Mozza's culinary artistry, combining the delicate tenderness of quail with the savory allure of pancetta and the luscious drizzle of balsamic glaze. Fire-kissed to perfection, this dish is a celebration of bold ingredients and meticulous technique, bringing the spirit of Mozza's renowned menu straight to your home kitchen.

Serving: Ideal for an intimate dinner for four or as an elegant appetizer for a larger gathering.
Preparation Time: 20 minutes
Ready Time: 1 hour

Ingredients:
- 8 quails, cleaned and halved
- 8 slices of pancetta
- 1/2 cup balsamic vinegar
- 1/4 cup honey
- 2 tablespoons olive oil
- 2 cloves garlic, minced
- 1 teaspoon fresh rosemary, finely chopped
- Salt and pepper to taste

Instructions:
1. Prepare the Quail:
- Rinse the quail under cold water and pat them dry with paper towels.
- Season the quail with salt, pepper, and minced garlic. Drizzle with olive oil and ensure they are well-coated.
2. Wrap with Pancetta:
- Carefully wrap each quail half with a slice of pancetta, ensuring it is securely wrapped around the meat.
3. Wood-Grilling:
- Preheat your wood grill to medium-high heat.
- Place the quail on the grill grates, cooking for about 5-7 minutes per side or until the pancetta is crispy, and the quail is cooked through.
4. Balsamic Glaze:
- In a small saucepan, combine balsamic vinegar and honey. Simmer over medium heat until the mixture thickens to a glaze consistency.
- Remove from heat and set aside.

5. Finishing Touch:
- Brush the wood-grilled quail with the prepared balsamic glaze, ensuring a generous coating on each piece.
- Sprinkle fresh rosemary over the quail for a burst of herbal fragrance.
6. Serve:
- Arrange the wood-grilled quail on a platter, drizzling any remaining balsamic glaze over the top.
- Serve hot, allowing your guests to savor the smoky, savory goodness.

Nutrition Information:
Note: Nutritional values are approximate and may vary based on specific ingredients used.
- Calories: 320 per serving
- Protein: 28g
- Carbohydrates: 12g
- Fat: 18g
- Fiber: 1g

Elevate your dining experience with the Wood-Grilled Quail, a culinary gem inspired by the inventive menu of Nancy Silverton's Mozza restaurant. Enjoy the harmony of flavors that dance on your palate, embodying the spirit of Mozza's commitment to exceptional ingredients and culinary expertise.

64. Prosciutto and Figs with Ricotta and Honey

Indulge your senses with the exquisite combination of flavors in this dish inspired by the renowned Nancy Silverton's Mozza restaurant. Prosciutto and Figs with Ricotta and Honey is a sophisticated yet simple dish that brings together the salty richness of prosciutto, the sweetness of ripe figs, the creamy texture of ricotta, and the golden drizzle of honey. It's a culinary symphony that captures the essence of Mozza's menu, elevating your dining experience to new heights.

Serving: Ideal for 4 servings.
Preparation Time: 15 minutes
Ready Time: 15 minutes

Ingredients:

- 8 slices of high-quality prosciutto
- 8 ripe figs, quartered
- 1 cup fresh ricotta cheese
- 4 tablespoons honey
- Freshly ground black pepper, to taste
- Fresh mint leaves for garnish

Instructions:
1. Prepare the Ingredients:
- Lay out the prosciutto slices on a serving platter.
- Wash and quarter the ripe figs, setting them aside.
- Spoon the ricotta onto the platter, creating small mounds alongside the prosciutto.
2. Assemble the Dish:
- Take a quartered fig and place it on each slice of prosciutto.
- Drizzle honey over the figs and ricotta, ensuring a generous coating.
- Sprinkle freshly ground black pepper over the entire platter for a hint of spice.
3. Garnish:
- Garnish the dish with fresh mint leaves, adding a pop of color and a hint of herbal freshness.
4. Serve:
- Serve immediately to enjoy the contrasting textures and flavors at their peak.

Nutrition Information:
Note: Nutrition information is approximate and may vary based on specific ingredients used.
- Calories per serving: 250
- Total Fat: 15g
- Saturated Fat: 8g
- Trans Fat: 0g
- Cholesterol: 45mg
- Sodium: 600mg
- Total Carbohydrates: 25g
- Dietary Fiber: 4g
- Sugars: 20g
- Protein: 10g

Elevate your dining experience with the Prosciutto and Figs with Ricotta and Honey—a dish that embodies the sophistication and culinary excellence of Nancy Silverton's Mozza restaurant.

65. Wood-Roasted Brussels Sprouts with Pancetta and Parmesan

Elevate your taste buds with the exquisite flavors of Nancy Silverton's Mozza restaurant-inspired dish—Wood-Roasted Brussels Sprouts with Pancetta and Parmesan. This delightful recipe captures the essence of Mozza's culinary excellence, combining the robust smokiness of wood-roasted Brussels sprouts with the savory richness of pancetta and the nutty depth of Parmesan. An irresistible medley of textures and tastes awaits you in this simple yet sophisticated side dish.

Serving: 4 servings
Preparation Time: 15 minutes
Ready Time: 40 minutes

Ingredients:
- 1 lb Brussels sprouts, trimmed and halved
- 3 oz pancetta, diced
- 2 tbsp olive oil
- Salt and pepper, to taste
- 1/4 cup freshly grated Parmesan cheese
- 2 tbsp balsamic glaze (optional, for drizzling)

Instructions:
1. Preheat your oven to 400°F (200°C). If you have a wood-burning oven or grill, preheat it for an authentic wood-roasted flavor.
2. In a large mixing bowl, toss the halved Brussels sprouts with olive oil, salt, and pepper until well coated.
3. Spread the Brussels sprouts evenly on a baking sheet or a roasting pan. If using a wood-burning oven or grill, place them directly on the grill grates.
4. Roast the Brussels sprouts in the preheated oven (or on the grill) for 25-30 minutes, or until they are tender and have a slightly charred

appearance. Toss them halfway through the cooking time for even roasting.
5. While the Brussels sprouts are roasting, in a medium skillet over medium heat, sauté the diced pancetta until it becomes crispy and golden brown.
6. Once the Brussels sprouts are done, transfer them to a serving platter. Sprinkle the crispy pancetta over the top.
7. Finish by generously grating Parmesan cheese over the Brussels sprouts and pancetta. For an extra touch, drizzle with balsamic glaze if desired.
8. Serve immediately, and savor the delightful combination of wood-roasted Brussels sprouts, savory pancetta, and the richness of Parmesan.

Nutrition Information:
(Per serving)
- Calories: 210
- Fat: 14g
- Saturated Fat: 4g
- Cholesterol: 15mg
- Sodium: 420mg
- Carbohydrates: 15g
- Fiber: 6g
- Sugar: 3g
- Protein: 9g

Enjoy this Mozza-inspired dish as a side that steals the spotlight, bringing a taste of culinary sophistication to your table.

66. Margherita Pizza with Mortadella and Pistachio

Indulge in the exquisite flavors inspired by Nancy Silverton's iconic Mozza restaurant with this delectable Margherita Pizza topped with the richness of Mortadella and the crunch of pistachios. A harmonious blend of classic and innovative, this pizza is a celebration of quality ingredients and culinary finesse. Follow the simple steps below to recreate the magic of Mozza in your own kitchen.

Serving: Makes 1 large pizza (approximately 8 slices)
Preparation Time: 20 minutes

Ready Time: 15 minutes (plus dough rising time)

Ingredients:
- 1 pizza dough (store-bought or homemade)
- 1/2 cup pizza sauce
- 1 1/2 cups fresh mozzarella, sliced
- 1/4 cup Parmesan cheese, grated
- 1/4 cup fresh basil leaves, torn
- 4-6 slices Mortadella, torn into pieces
- 1/3 cup pistachios, shelled and chopped
- Olive oil, for drizzling
- Salt and pepper, to taste

Instructions:
1. Preheat your oven to the highest temperature it can reach (usually around 475-500°F or 245-260°C). If you have a pizza stone, place it in the oven during the preheating.
2. Roll out the pizza dough on a lightly floured surface to your desired thickness. If you have a pizza peel, transfer the dough onto it; otherwise, use a sheet of parchment paper.
3. Spread the pizza sauce evenly over the dough, leaving a small border for the crust.
4. Arrange the fresh mozzarella slices on top of the sauce, followed by the torn Mortadella pieces.
5. Sprinkle the grated Parmesan over the pizza and season with salt and pepper to taste.
6. If you're using a pizza stone, carefully transfer the pizza onto the preheated stone in the oven. If not, place the parchment paper directly on the oven rack.
7. Bake for about 10-12 minutes or until the crust is golden and the cheese is melted and bubbly.
8. Once out of the oven, scatter torn fresh basil leaves and chopped pistachios over the hot pizza.
9. Drizzle with olive oil for added richness and flavor.
10. Allow the pizza to cool for a few minutes before slicing.

Nutrition Information:
(Per Slice - based on 8 slices)
- Calories: 280
- Total Fat: 14g

- Saturated Fat: 5g
- Trans Fat: 0g
- Cholesterol: 30mg
- Sodium: 580mg
- Total Carbohydrates: 26g
- Dietary Fiber: 2g
- Sugars: 2g
- Protein: 14g

Note: Nutrition information is approximate and may vary based on specific ingredients used. Adjustments can be made based on dietary preferences and requirements. Enjoy your slice of Mozza-inspired heaven!

67. Burrata with Roasted Butternut Squash and Sage

Indulge in the exquisite flavors of Nancy Silverton's Mozza restaurant with this delightful recipe for Burrata with Roasted Butternut Squash and Sage. This dish perfectly captures the essence of Mozza's culinary finesse, combining creamy burrata with the earthy sweetness of roasted butternut squash and the aromatic touch of sage. Elevate your dining experience with this elegant and delectable appetizer that embodies the essence of Mozza's menu.

Serving: 4 servings
Preparation Time: 15 minutes
Ready Time: 45 minutes

Ingredients:
- 1 butternut squash, peeled, seeded, and diced
- 2 tablespoons olive oil
- Salt and pepper, to taste
- 1 tablespoon fresh sage leaves, chopped
- 1 teaspoon honey
- 1 tablespoon balsamic glaze
- 1 burrata cheese ball (about 8 ounces)
- Balsamic reduction, for drizzling (optional)
- Toasted baguette slices, for serving

Instructions:

1. Preheat the Oven:

Preheat your oven to 400°F (200°C).

2. Roast Butternut Squash:

- Place the diced butternut squash on a baking sheet.
- Drizzle with olive oil and season with salt and pepper.
- Toss the squash to coat evenly and spread it out in a single layer.
- Roast in the preheated oven for 30-35 minutes or until the squash is tender and golden brown, stirring halfway through.
- In the last 5 minutes of roasting, sprinkle the chopped sage over the squash and continue to roast until the sage is crispy.

3. Finish the Butternut Squash:

- Remove the roasted butternut squash from the oven and drizzle with honey and balsamic glaze. Toss gently to combine.

4. Prepare the Burrata:

- Place the burrata on a serving platter.
- Make a small incision in the center of the burrata to allow the creamy interior to spill out.

5. Assemble the Dish:

- Spoon the roasted butternut squash mixture around the burrata.
- Optionally, drizzle with balsamic reduction for extra richness.
- Serve with toasted baguette slices for a delightful combination of flavors and textures.

6. Serve and Enjoy:

Indulge in the harmonious blend of creamy burrata, roasted butternut squash, and aromatic sage. Spread the mixture on the toasted baguette slices for a perfect bite.

Nutrition Information:

(Per Serving)

- Calories: 280
- Total Fat: 20g
- Saturated Fat: 8g
- Cholesterol: 40mg
- Sodium: 180mg
- Total Carbohydrates: 22g
- Dietary Fiber: 4g
- Sugars: 5g
- Protein: 9g

Note: Nutrition information is approximate and may vary based on specific ingredients and portion sizes.

68. Grilled Sardines with Lemon and Parsley

Indulge in the culinary excellence of Nancy Silverton's Mozza restaurant with our delightful recipe for Grilled Sardines with Lemon and Parsley. This dish captures the essence of Mozza's commitment to fresh, vibrant flavors that transport your taste buds to the heart of Mediterranean cuisine. Savor the simplicity of this recipe, allowing the natural flavors of the sardines to shine, enhanced by the zesty brightness of lemon and the aromatic touch of fresh parsley.

Serving: 4 servings
Preparation Time: 15 minutes
Ready Time: 25 minutes

Ingredients:
- 12 fresh sardines, cleaned and gutted
- 2 lemons, thinly sliced
- 1/4 cup fresh parsley, finely chopped
- 1/4 cup extra-virgin olive oil
- Salt and pepper to taste

Instructions:
1. Preheat the grill to medium-high heat.
2. In a small bowl, whisk together the extra-virgin olive oil, chopped parsley, salt, and pepper to create a flavorful marinade.
3. Place the cleaned sardines on a tray and generously brush them with the prepared marinade, ensuring they are well-coated.
4. Lay lemon slices directly on the preheated grill and cook for about 2-3 minutes on each side or until they develop a light char. Set aside.
5. Carefully place the marinated sardines on the grill, cooking for approximately 4-5 minutes per side or until they are cooked through and have a delicious smoky flavor.
6. Arrange the grilled sardines on a serving platter, and garnish with the grilled lemon slices.

7. Drizzle any remaining marinade over the top for an extra burst of flavor.
8. Serve the Grilled Sardines with Lemon and Parsley alongside your favorite Mediterranean sides or a crisp green salad.

Nutrition Information:
Note: Nutritional values are approximate and may vary based on specific ingredients used.
- Calories: 220 per serving
- Protein: 25g
- Fat: 12g
- Carbohydrates: 3g
- Fiber: 1g
- Sugar: 1g
- Sodium: 350mg

Elevate your dining experience with this Mozza-inspired dish, celebrating the simplicity and bold flavors that define Nancy Silverton's culinary philosophy.

69. Radicchio and Endive Salad with Orange and Hazelnuts

Indulge your palate in the vibrant flavors of Nancy Silverton's Mozza restaurant with this refreshing Radicchio and Endive Salad with Orange and Hazelnuts. A symphony of crisp radicchio and endive, citrusy orange segments, and the nutty crunch of hazelnuts, this salad embodies the culinary essence of Mozza's inventive and delightful menu.

Serving: 4 servings
Preparation Time: 15 minutes
Ready Time: 20 minutes

Ingredients:
- 1 head radicchio, thinly sliced
- 2 heads endive, chopped
- 2 oranges, peeled and segmented
- 1/2 cup hazelnuts, toasted and roughly chopped
- 2 tablespoons fresh parsley, chopped

For the Dressing:
- 3 tablespoons extra virgin olive oil
- 2 tablespoons orange juice
- 1 tablespoon red wine vinegar
- 1 teaspoon Dijon mustard
- Salt and pepper to taste

Instructions:
1. Prepare the Salad: In a large bowl, combine the sliced radicchio and chopped endive.
2. Add the Oranges: Gently fold in the orange segments, distributing them evenly throughout the salad.
3. Make the Dressing: In a small bowl, whisk together the olive oil, orange juice, red wine vinegar, Dijon mustard, salt, and pepper until well combined.
4. Dress the Salad: Drizzle the dressing over the salad and toss gently to coat the ingredients evenly.
5. Toast the Hazelnuts: In a dry skillet over medium heat, toast the hazelnuts until fragrant and lightly browned. Be sure to stir frequently to prevent burning.
6. Finish the Salad: Sprinkle the toasted hazelnuts over the salad, and garnish with fresh parsley.
7. Serve: Plate the salad and serve immediately to preserve the crispness of the greens and the crunch of the hazelnuts.

Nutrition Information:
Note: Nutritional values are approximate and may vary based on specific ingredients used.
- Calories: 180 per serving
- Total Fat: 14g
- Saturated Fat: 1.5g
- Trans Fat: 0g
- Cholesterol: 0mg
- Sodium: 120mg
- Total Carbohydrates: 13g
- Dietary Fiber: 5g
- Sugars: 6g
- Protein: 3g

Elevate your dining experience with this Radicchio and Endive Salad – a testament to the culinary finesse celebrated at Nancy Silverton's Mozza restaurant.

70. Spaghetti Carbonara with Pancetta and Pecorino

Indulge in the timeless Italian classic, inspired by the culinary mastery of Nancy Silverton's Mozza restaurant. Our Spaghetti Carbonara with Pancetta and Pecorino captures the essence of Mozza's exquisite menu, delivering a symphony of flavors that dance on your palate. This dish, rich with the robust taste of pancetta and the sharp kick of Pecorino, is a celebration of simplicity and sophistication.

Serving: This recipe serves 4.
Preparation Time: 15 minutes
Ready Time: 30 minutes

Ingredients:
- 400g spaghetti
- 200g pancetta, diced
- 4 large eggs
- 1 cup Pecorino Romano cheese, finely grated
- 1 cup Parmesan cheese, finely grated
- 3 cloves garlic, minced
- Freshly ground black pepper, to taste
- Salt, to taste
- Chopped fresh parsley, for garnish

Instructions:
1. Boil the Spaghetti: Cook the spaghetti in a large pot of salted boiling water until al dente. Reserve about 1 cup of pasta water before draining.
2. Cook Pancetta: In a large skillet over medium heat, cook the diced pancetta until it becomes crispy and golden brown. Add minced garlic to the pan and sauté until fragrant.
3. Prepare the Egg Mixture: In a bowl, whisk together the eggs, Pecorino Romano, and Parmesan cheeses until well combined.

4. Combine Ingredients: Once the spaghetti is cooked, add it to the skillet with the pancetta and garlic. Toss to combine, ensuring the pasta is well coated with the pancetta and garlic flavors.
5. Add Egg Mixture: Remove the skillet from heat and quickly pour the egg and cheese mixture over the spaghetti, tossing vigorously to create a creamy sauce. If needed, add reserved pasta water gradually to achieve the desired consistency.
6. Season and Garnish: Season with salt and freshly ground black pepper to taste. Garnish with chopped fresh parsley for a burst of color and freshness.
7. Serve: Divide the spaghetti carbonara among plates, ensuring each portion is generously coated with the luscious sauce.

Nutrition Information:
(Per Serving)
- Calories: 650
- Total Fat: 25g
- Saturated Fat: 12g
- Trans Fat: 0g
- Cholesterol: 230mg
- Sodium: 700mg
- Total Carbohydrates: 70g
- Dietary Fiber: 3g
- Sugars: 2g
- Protein: 35g

Embrace the spirit of Mozza's kitchen with this Spaghetti Carbonara – a dish that embodies the art of crafting simple ingredients into an extraordinary culinary experience.

71. Margherita Pizza with Arugula and Provolone

Indulge in the culinary magic inspired by the renowned Nancy Silverton's Mozza restaurant with our take on the classic Margherita Pizza. Elevating this beloved dish, we've added a twist by topping it with peppery arugula and luscious Provolone cheese. The result? A harmonious blend of flavors that pays homage to the sophisticated and comforting cuisine of Mozza.

Serving: 4 servings
Preparation Time: 20 minutes
Ready Time: 15 minutes (plus dough preparation time, if making from scratch)

Ingredients:
- 1 pound pizza dough (store-bought or homemade)
- 1/2 cup pizza sauce
- 8 ounces fresh mozzarella, thinly sliced
- 1 cup cherry tomatoes, halved
- 2 cups arugula, washed and dried
- 1/2 cup Provolone cheese, shredded
- 2 tablespoons extra-virgin olive oil
- Salt and black pepper to taste
- Fresh basil leaves for garnish (optional)

Instructions:
1. Preheat your oven to the highest temperature it can go, usually around 475-500°F (245-260°C).
2. Roll out the pizza dough on a floured surface to your desired thickness. If you prefer a thin crust, roll it out thinner.
3. Transfer the rolled-out dough to a pizza stone or a baking sheet.
4. Spread the pizza sauce evenly over the dough, leaving a small border around the edges for the crust.
5. Arrange the fresh mozzarella slices and halved cherry tomatoes on top of the sauce.
6. Sprinkle the shredded Provolone cheese over the pizza.
7. Season with salt and black pepper to taste.
8. Bake in the preheated oven for 12-15 minutes, or until the crust is golden and the cheese is melted and bubbly.
9. While the pizza is baking, toss the arugula with olive oil in a bowl.
10. Once the pizza is out of the oven, immediately top it with the arugula mixture.
11. Optional: Garnish with fresh basil leaves for an extra burst of flavor.
12. Slice and serve hot.

Nutrition Information:
(Per Serving)
- Calories: 450
- Fat: 20g

- Saturated Fat: 8g
- Cholesterol: 40mg
- Sodium: 900mg
- Carbohydrates: 50g
- Fiber: 3g
- Sugar: 4g
- Protein: 20g

Note: Nutrition information is approximate and may vary based on specific ingredients used.

72. Wood-Grilled Pork Ribs with Fennel Pollen and Chili

Indulge in the bold and flavorful essence of Nancy Silverton's Mozza restaurant with these Wood-Grilled Pork Ribs adorned with the aromatic touch of fennel pollen and a hint of chili. This dish captures the essence of Mozza's commitment to quality ingredients and expertly crafted flavors, delivering a dining experience that elevates the humble pork rib to new heights. The wood-grilling technique imparts a smoky depth, while fennel pollen adds a unique, fragrant note, creating a symphony of taste that echoes the renowned culinary expertise of Mozza.

Serving: 4 servings
Preparation Time: 15 minutes
Ready Time: 3 hours (including marination and grilling)

Ingredients:
- 2 racks of pork ribs (about 3 pounds each)
- 2 tablespoons fennel pollen
- 1 tablespoon chili powder
- 1 tablespoon smoked paprika
- 2 teaspoons garlic powder
- 2 teaspoons onion powder
- 1 teaspoon cayenne pepper
- Salt and black pepper, to taste
- Olive oil for brushing

Instructions:

1. Prepare the Ribs:
- Rinse the pork ribs under cold water and pat them dry with paper towels.
- Remove the thin membrane from the back of the ribs for better flavor absorption.
2. Marinate the Ribs:
- In a small bowl, combine fennel pollen, chili powder, smoked paprika, garlic powder, onion powder, cayenne pepper, salt, and black pepper to create a dry rub.
- Rub the spice mixture evenly over both sides of the ribs, pressing it into the meat.
- Place the ribs in a large dish, cover with plastic wrap, and refrigerate for at least 2 hours or preferably overnight to allow the flavors to penetrate.
3. Preheat the Grill:
- Prepare a wood-fired grill for indirect grilling at medium heat (about 300°F/150°C).
4. Grill the Ribs:
- Brush the ribs with olive oil before placing them on the grill.
- Grill the ribs over indirect heat, turning occasionally, until the meat is tender and has a smoky char, approximately 2 to 2.5 hours.
5. Rest and Serve:
- Allow the ribs to rest for a few minutes before slicing into individual servings.
- Serve the wood-grilled pork ribs with your favorite sides, perhaps inspired by the Mozza restaurant menu.

Nutrition Information:
(Per serving, based on a 4-serving yield)
- Calories: XXX
- Total Fat: XXg
- Saturated Fat: XXg
- Cholesterol: XXXmg
- Sodium: XXXmg
- Total Carbohydrates: XXg
- Dietary Fiber: XXg
- Sugars: XXg
- Protein: XXg

Elevate your home cooking experience with these Wood-Grilled Pork Ribs, a tribute to the culinary artistry found at Nancy Silverton's Mozza restaurant. Enjoy the robust flavors and tender texture that make this dish a standout on any dining table.

73. Burrata with Roasted Peaches, Prosciutto, and Mint

Indulge in the culinary elegance of Nancy Silverton's Mozza restaurant with this exquisite dish—Burrata with Roasted Peaches, Prosciutto, and Mint. Elevate your dining experience with the perfect harmony of creamy burrata, sweet roasted peaches, salty prosciutto, and the refreshing touch of mint. This recipe captures the essence of Mozza's sophisticated yet approachable menu, bringing a burst of flavors to your table.

Serving: Serves 4
Preparation Time: 15 minutes
Ready Time: 30 minutes

Ingredients:
- 2 ripe peaches, sliced into wedges
- 1 tablespoon olive oil
- 1 teaspoon honey
- Salt and pepper to taste
- 1 pound burrata cheese
- 4 slices prosciutto
- Fresh mint leaves for garnish

Instructions:
1. Preheat the Oven:
Preheat your oven to 400°F (200°C).
2. Roast the Peaches:
a. In a bowl, toss the peach wedges with olive oil, honey, salt, and pepper.
b. Spread the peaches on a baking sheet in a single layer.
c. Roast in the preheated oven for 15-20 minutes or until the peaches are caramelized and tender.
3. Prepare the Burrata:

Place the burrata on a serving platter, allowing it to come to room temperature for optimal creaminess.
4. Assemble the Dish:
a. Arrange the roasted peach wedges around the burrata.
b. Drape slices of prosciutto over the burrata and peaches.
5. Finish with Mint:
Scatter fresh mint leaves over the dish for a burst of aromatic freshness.
6. Serve:
Serve immediately, allowing guests to scoop up a perfect bite of burrata, roasted peaches, prosciutto, and mint.

Nutrition Information:
Note: Nutritional values are approximate and may vary based on specific ingredients used.
- Calories per serving: 350
- Total Fat: 25g
- Saturated Fat: 12g
- Cholesterol: 60mg
- Sodium: 600mg
- Total Carbohydrates: 15g
- Dietary Fiber: 2g
- Sugars: 12g
- Protein: 18g

Enjoy the delicate dance of flavors in this Burrata with Roasted Peaches, Prosciutto, and Mint—a culinary masterpiece inspired by the renowned Nancy Silverton's Mozza restaurant. Perfect for a light, sophisticated appetizer or a delightful addition to your next gathering.

74. Grilled Octopus Salad with Fingerling Potatoes and Green Beans

Indulge your palate in the exquisite flavors inspired by the renowned Nancy Silverton's Mozza restaurant with our Grilled Octopus Salad. This dish perfectly captures the essence of Mozza's culinary finesse, combining tender grilled octopus with the earthy richness of fingerling potatoes and the vibrant crunch of green beans. A symphony of textures and tastes awaits you in this delightful salad that seamlessly marries

Mediterranean influences with the California freshness that Mozza is celebrated for.

Serving: 4 servings
Preparation time: 20 minutes
Ready time: 1 hour

Ingredients:
- 1 lb octopus, cleaned
- 1 lb fingerling potatoes, halved
- 1/2 lb green beans, trimmed
- 1/4 cup extra-virgin olive oil
- 3 cloves garlic, minced
- 1 teaspoon dried oregano
- Salt and pepper to taste
- Zest of 1 lemon
- 2 tablespoons fresh lemon juice
- 1/4 cup fresh parsley, chopped
- 1/4 cup Kalamata olives, pitted and sliced
- 2 tablespoons red wine vinegar
- 1 teaspoon Dijon mustard
- Mixed salad greens for serving

Instructions:
1. Preheat the Grill:
- Preheat your grill to medium-high heat.
2. Prepare Octopus:
- If the octopus hasn't been cleaned, remove the beak and be sure to clean the interior. Pat it dry with paper towels.
- In a bowl, mix olive oil, minced garlic, oregano, salt, and pepper. Brush this mixture over the octopus.
3. Grill Octopus:
- Grill the octopus for about 4-5 minutes per side or until it's tender and has a nice char. Cooking time may vary based on the size of the octopus.
4. Boil Potatoes and Green Beans:
- While grilling, boil the halved fingerling potatoes and green beans in salted water until they are tender but still have a slight bite. Drain and set aside.
5. Prepare Dressing:

- In a small bowl, whisk together lemon zest, lemon juice, red wine vinegar, Dijon mustard, and salt and pepper to taste.
6. Assemble Salad:
- In a large bowl, combine the grilled octopus, boiled potatoes, green beans, olives, and chopped parsley.
- Pour the dressing over the salad and toss gently to coat everything evenly.
7. Serve:
- Arrange a bed of mixed salad greens on each plate and top with the grilled octopus mixture.
8. Garnish and Enjoy:
- Drizzle a bit more olive oil over the top, sprinkle with additional chopped parsley, and serve immediately.

Nutrition Information (per serving):
- Calories: 350
- Protein: 25g
- Carbohydrates: 20g
- Fat: 20g
- Fiber: 5g

Elevate your dining experience with this Grilled Octopus Salad, a tribute to the culinary brilliance of Nancy Silverton's Mozza restaurant. Each bite is a celebration of freshness, flavor, and the artistry that defines Mozza's exceptional menu.

75. Shaved Brussels Sprouts Pizza with Fontina and Pancetta

Indulge your taste buds in the culinary wonders inspired by the famed Mozza restaurant, as we present the Shaved Brussels Sprouts Pizza with Fontina and Pancetta. This delectable pizza pays homage to the inventive spirit and bold flavors championed by Nancy Silverton. The combination of shaved Brussels sprouts, creamy Fontina cheese, and savory pancetta creates a symphony of tastes that will elevate your pizza experience to new heights. Prepare to embark on a gastronomic journey that mirrors the excellence of Mozza's renowned menu.

Serving: Makes 1 pizza (approximately 8 slices)

Preparation Time: 20 minutes
Ready Time: 30 minutes

Ingredients:
- 1 pizza dough (store-bought or homemade)
- 1 cup shaved Brussels sprouts
- 1 cup shredded Fontina cheese
- 4 ounces pancetta, thinly sliced
- 2 tablespoons olive oil
- Salt and pepper to taste
- 1/4 cup grated Parmesan cheese
- Red pepper flakes (optional, for added spice)

Instructions:
1. Preheat your oven to 475°F (245°C). If you have a pizza stone, place it in the oven to heat.
2. On a floured surface, roll out the pizza dough to your desired thickness.
3. In a skillet over medium heat, sauté the shaved Brussels sprouts in olive oil until they are just tender, about 3-4 minutes. Season with salt and pepper to taste.
4. If using a pizza stone, carefully transfer the rolled-out dough onto a pizza peel or an inverted baking sheet. If not using a pizza stone, place the rolled-out dough directly onto a parchment-lined baking sheet.
5. Sprinkle the shredded Fontina cheese evenly over the pizza dough, leaving a small border around the edges.
6. Distribute the sautéed Brussels sprouts and pancetta slices over the cheese.
7. Drizzle a bit of olive oil over the top and transfer the pizza to the preheated oven or onto the pizza stone. Bake for 12-15 minutes or until the crust is golden and the cheese is bubbly and slightly browned.
8. Remove the pizza from the oven and sprinkle with grated Parmesan cheese. If you enjoy a hint of spice, add red pepper flakes to taste.
9. Allow the pizza to cool for a few minutes before slicing.

Nutrition Information:
Note: Nutritional values may vary based on specific ingredients used and portion sizes.
- Calories: ~280 per slice
- Fat: ~12g

- Saturated Fat: ~5g
- Cholesterol: ~20mg
- Sodium: ~550mg
- Carbohydrates: ~30g
- Fiber: ~2g
- Sugars: ~1g
- Protein: ~12g

Embrace the bold flavors and innovative combinations of Mozza with this Shaved Brussels Sprouts Pizza—a culinary masterpiece that captures the essence of Nancy Silverton's culinary expertise. Enjoy!

76. Tomato and Stracciatella Salad with Basil and Balsamic

Indulge in the vibrant flavors of Nancy Silverton's Mozza restaurant with this Tomato and Stracciatella Salad, a delightful fusion of freshness and creaminess. Inspired by the restaurant's commitment to quality ingredients, this salad showcases the simplicity of ripe tomatoes, luscious Stracciatella cheese, fragrant basil, and a drizzle of balsamic glaze. It's a celebration of seasonal produce and the art of combining flavors to create a dish that's both satisfying and refreshing.

Serving: 4 servings
Preparation Time: 15 minutes
Ready Time: 15 minutes

Ingredients:
- 4 large ripe tomatoes, sliced
- 200g Stracciatella cheese
- 1/2 cup fresh basil leaves, torn
- 2 tablespoons balsamic glaze
- Salt and pepper to taste
- Extra virgin olive oil for drizzling

Instructions:
1. Prepare the Tomatoes:
- Wash and slice the tomatoes into 1/4-inch rounds. Arrange them on a serving platter, slightly overlapping for a visually appealing presentation.

2. Add Stracciatella:
- Distribute the Stracciatella cheese over the sliced tomatoes. Gently tear the cheese and distribute it evenly, allowing it to meld with the tomatoes.
3. Sprinkle Basil:
- Scatter torn basil leaves over the salad, ensuring a balance of color and freshness. The aromatic basil adds a layer of herbaceous flavor to the dish.
4. Season and Drizzle:
- Season the salad with salt and pepper to taste. Drizzle the balsamic glaze generously over the tomatoes and Stracciatella, adding a sweet and tangy element to the ensemble.
5. Finish with Olive Oil:
- Just before serving, drizzle extra virgin olive oil over the salad. This enhances the richness of the Stracciatella and ties together the flavors.
6. Serve Immediately:
- This salad is best enjoyed immediately to preserve the freshness of the ingredients. Serve as a light lunch, a refreshing appetizer, or as a side dish to complement your main course.

Nutrition Information:
Note: Nutritional values are approximate and may vary based on specific ingredients used.
- Calories per serving: 200 kcal
- Total Fat: 15g
- Saturated Fat: 8g
- Trans Fat: 0g
- Cholesterol: 40mg
- Sodium: 300mg
- Total Carbohydrates: 10g
- Dietary Fiber: 2g
- Sugars: 6g
- Protein: 8g

Elevate your dining experience with the vibrant flavors of this Tomato and Stracciatella Salad inspired by the culinary excellence of Nancy Silverton's Mozza restaurant. Each bite is a symphony of textures and tastes, celebrating the essence of fresh, high-quality ingredients.

77. Wood-Grilled Lamb Sausage with Eggplant and Yogurt

Indulge in the rustic charm and bold flavors of Nancy Silverton's Mozza restaurant with our Wood-Grilled Lamb Sausage paired with smoky Eggplant and luscious Yogurt. This recipe captures the essence of Mozza's culinary excellence, bringing together the earthy richness of wood-grilled lamb, the velvety texture of roasted eggplant, and the tangy creaminess of yogurt. It's a symphony of tastes that pays homage to the restaurant's commitment to quality ingredients and inventive combinations.

Serving: 4 servings
Preparation Time: 20 minutes
Ready Time: 40 minutes

Ingredients:
- 1 lb lamb sausages
- 2 medium-sized eggplants, sliced into rounds
- 1 cup Greek yogurt
- 2 tablespoons olive oil
- 2 cloves garlic, minced
- 1 teaspoon ground cumin
- 1 teaspoon smoked paprika
- Salt and pepper to taste
- Fresh mint leaves for garnish

Instructions:
1. Preheat the wood grill to medium-high heat.
2. In a bowl, combine olive oil, minced garlic, cumin, smoked paprika, salt, and pepper. Brush the eggplant slices with this mixture, ensuring they are evenly coated.
3. Grill the lamb sausages, turning occasionally, until they are cooked through and have a delicious char, approximately 15-20 minutes.
4. Simultaneously, place the seasoned eggplant slices on the grill and cook for about 3-4 minutes per side, or until they are tender and have distinctive grill marks.
5. While the sausages and eggplants are grilling, mix the Greek yogurt with a pinch of salt.

6. Once the lamb sausages are cooked, remove them from the grill and let them rest for a few minutes.
7. To serve, arrange the grilled lamb sausages and eggplant slices on a platter. Add dollops of seasoned Greek yogurt on the side and garnish with fresh mint leaves.
8. Serve this Wood-Grilled Lamb Sausage with Eggplant and Yogurt dish hot, allowing guests to savor the medley of flavors with each bite.

Nutrition Information:
(Per serving)
- Calories: 450
- Protein: 22g
- Fat: 35g
- Carbohydrates: 15g
- Fiber: 6g
- Sugar: 8g
- Sodium: 700mg

Elevate your dining experience with this Mozza-inspired creation, where each element contributes to a harmonious and memorable meal.

78. Prosciutto and Melon Pizza with Arugula

Indulge your palate in the symphony of flavors with our Prosciutto and Melon Pizza with Arugula, inspired by the culinary mastery of Nancy Silverton's Mozza restaurant. This exquisite pizza combines the richness of prosciutto, the sweetness of melon, and the peppery kick of arugula to create a harmonious medley that will transport you to the heart of Mozza's celebrated menu.

Serving: Makes one 12-inch pizza, serving 4.
Preparation Time: 20 minutes
Ready Time: 15 minutes (plus dough preparation time)

Ingredients:
- 1 pound pizza dough (store-bought or homemade)
- 1/4 cup olive oil
- 1 clove garlic, minced
- 1 1/2 cups shredded mozzarella cheese

- 6 slices prosciutto
- 1 cup cantaloupe or honeydew melon, thinly sliced
- 2 cups arugula, washed and dried
- 1/4 cup shaved Parmesan cheese
- Balsamic glaze for drizzling (optional)
- Salt and black pepper to taste

Instructions:

1. Preheat the Oven:
Preheat your oven to 475°F (245°C). If you have a pizza stone, place it in the oven during preheating.
2. Roll Out the Dough:
Roll out the pizza dough on a lightly floured surface to your desired thickness. If you have a pizza peel, transfer the rolled-out dough onto it.
3. Prepare the Olive Oil Mixture:
In a small bowl, mix the olive oil and minced garlic. Brush the olive oil mixture evenly over the surface of the pizza dough.
4. Add the Cheese and Prosciutto:
Sprinkle the shredded mozzarella evenly over the oiled dough. Place the prosciutto slices on top of the cheese.
5. Bake the Pizza:
If using a pizza stone, carefully transfer the pizza onto the preheated stone in the oven. If not using a stone, place the pizza on a baking sheet. Bake for 12-15 minutes or until the crust is golden and the cheese is melted and bubbly.
6. Add the Melon and Arugula:
Remove the pizza from the oven and immediately scatter the thinly sliced melon over the hot cheese. Top with fresh arugula and shaved Parmesan. Season with salt and black pepper to taste.
7. Drizzle with Balsamic Glaze (Optional):
For an extra burst of flavor, drizzle balsamic glaze over the finished pizza.
8. Serve and Enjoy:
Slice the pizza and serve it hot. Revel in the unique blend of sweet and savory, crisp and creamy.

Nutrition Information:

Note: Nutritional values may vary based on specific ingredients and portion sizes.
- Calories per serving: approximately 400 kcal

- Protein: 15g
- Carbohydrates: 30g
- Fat: 25g
- Fiber: 2g
- Sugar: 4g
- Sodium: 800mg

Elevate your pizza experience with this Prosciutto and Melon creation, a tribute to the culinary finesse of Nancy Silverton's Mozza.

79. Grilled Asparagus with Soft Egg and Parmesan

Indulge in the culinary elegance of Nancy Silverton's Mozza restaurant with this delectable recipe for Grilled Asparagus with Soft Egg and Parmesan. This dish is a celebration of simple yet sophisticated flavors, perfectly capturing the essence of Mozza's renowned menu. The vibrant green asparagus, creamy soft egg, and rich Parmesan cheese come together in a harmonious dance of textures and tastes. Elevate your dining experience with this inspired creation that pays homage to the exquisite culinary legacy of Mozza.

Serving: Ideal for 4 servings.
Preparation Time: 15 minutes
Ready Time: 25 minutes

Ingredients:
- 1 bunch of fresh asparagus, woody ends trimmed
- 4 large eggs
- 1/2 cup freshly grated Parmesan cheese
- 2 tablespoons extra-virgin olive oil
- Salt and freshly ground black pepper, to taste

Instructions:
1. Preheat the grill to medium-high heat.
2. Drizzle the trimmed asparagus with olive oil and season with salt and pepper. Toss to coat evenly.
3. Place the asparagus on the preheated grill and cook for 3-4 minutes, turning occasionally, until they are tender and have a slight char.

4. While the asparagus is grilling, bring a pot of water to a gentle simmer. Carefully crack the eggs into the simmering water, one at a time, and poach for about 3 minutes until the whites are set but the yolks remain soft.
5. Remove the asparagus from the grill and arrange them on serving plates.
6. Place a poached egg on top of each asparagus bunch, allowing the yolk to gently cascade over the spears.
7. Sprinkle freshly grated Parmesan cheese generously over the asparagus and eggs.
8. Finish with a drizzle of extra-virgin olive oil and a pinch of black pepper.
9. Serve immediately, allowing guests to enjoy the creamy texture of the soft egg combined with the crispness of grilled asparagus and the nuttiness of Parmesan.

Nutrition Information:
(Per Serving)
- Calories: 220
- Protein: 12g
- Fat: 18g
- Carbohydrates: 5g
- Fiber: 2g
- Sugar: 2g
- Sodium: 280mg

Experience the culinary magic of Mozza in the comfort of your own home with this Grilled Asparagus with Soft Egg and Parmesan recipe.

80. Burrata with Roasted Grapes, Almonds, and Honey

Indulge your senses in the culinary poetry inspired by the renowned Nancy Silverton's Mozza restaurant. This recipe captures the essence of Mozza's refined yet rustic charm, blending the creaminess of burrata with the rich sweetness of roasted grapes, the crunch of almonds, and the golden drizzle of honey. A harmonious symphony of flavors that elevates the simple joy of dining into a sublime experience.

Serving: 4 servings
Preparation Time: 15 minutes
Ready Time: 30 minutes

Ingredients:
- 4 balls of fresh burrata
- 2 cups red seedless grapes, washed and stems removed
- 1/2 cup whole almonds, toasted and coarsely chopped
- 4 tablespoons honey
- 2 tablespoons extra virgin olive oil
- Freshly ground black pepper, to taste
- Flaky sea salt, to taste
- Fresh basil leaves, for garnish (optional)

Instructions:
1. Preheat the oven:
Preheat your oven to 400°F (200°C).
2. Roast the grapes:
Spread the grapes on a baking sheet, drizzle with 1 tablespoon of olive oil, and toss to coat. Roast in the preheated oven for about 15-20 minutes or until the grapes are slightly caramelized and soft. Remove from the oven and let them cool slightly.
3. Prepare the almonds:
While the grapes are roasting, toast the almonds in a dry skillet over medium heat until they become golden and fragrant. Coarsely chop them and set aside.
4. Assemble the burrata:
Place each ball of burrata on a serving plate. Cut a small slit into each burrata to reveal the creamy interior.
5. Arrange the elements:
Scatter the roasted grapes and chopped almonds around the burrata. Drizzle each plate with 1 tablespoon of honey and the remaining olive oil. Season with freshly ground black pepper and a sprinkle of flaky sea salt.
6. Garnish:
Garnish with fresh basil leaves if desired, adding a touch of herbaceous aroma.
7. Serve:

Serve immediately, allowing guests to experience the delightful contrast of creamy burrata, sweet roasted grapes, crunchy almonds, and the luscious honey drizzle.

Nutrition Information:
(Per serving)
- Calories: 380
- Total Fat: 28g
- Saturated Fat: 12g
- Trans Fat: 0g
- Cholesterol: 60mg
- Sodium: 250mg
- Total Carbohydrates: 25g
- Dietary Fiber: 3g
- Sugars: 20g
- Protein: 15g

Note: Nutrition information is approximate and may vary based on specific ingredients used.

81. Wood-Grilled Swordfish with Tomato and Olive Relish

Indulge in the culinary magic inspired by Nancy Silverton's renowned Mozza restaurant with this tantalizing recipe for Wood-Grilled Swordfish with Tomato and Olive Relish. Elevate your dining experience with the perfect harmony of smoky swordfish, complemented by the vibrant flavors of a zesty tomato and olive relish. This dish captures the essence of Mozza's commitment to fresh, high-quality ingredients and inventive combinations that awaken the senses.

Serving: 4 servings
Preparation Time: 20 minutes
Ready Time: 30 minutes

Ingredients:
- 4 swordfish steaks (6 ounces each)
- 2 tablespoons olive oil
- Salt and black pepper to taste

For the Tomato and Olive Relish:
- 1 cup cherry tomatoes, halved
- 1/2 cup Kalamata olives, pitted and chopped
- 1/4 cup red onion, finely diced
- 2 tablespoons fresh parsley, chopped
- 2 tablespoons extra-virgin olive oil
- 1 tablespoon red wine vinegar
- Salt and black pepper to taste

Instructions:
1. Preheat the Grill:
Preheat your wood-fired grill to medium-high heat.
2. Prepare the Swordfish:
- Brush the swordfish steaks with olive oil and season generously with salt and black pepper.
3. Grill the Swordfish:
- Place the seasoned swordfish steaks on the preheated grill. Cook for approximately 4-5 minutes per side, or until the fish is opaque and easily flakes with a fork. The wood-grilled flavor will impart a delightful smokiness to the swordfish.
4. Make the Tomato and Olive Relish:
- In a bowl, combine the halved cherry tomatoes, chopped Kalamata olives, finely diced red onion, and fresh parsley.
- Drizzle extra-virgin olive oil and red wine vinegar over the mixture.
- Season with salt and black pepper to taste.
- Gently toss the ingredients until well combined.
5. Serve:
- Place the grilled swordfish steaks on individual plates.
- Spoon the tomato and olive relish generously over each swordfish steak.
6. Garnish and Enjoy:
- Garnish with additional fresh parsley, if desired.
- Serve immediately and relish in the exquisite blend of flavors.

Nutrition Information:
(Note: Nutritional values are approximate and may vary based on specific ingredients and serving sizes.)
- Calories: 350 per serving
- Protein: 30g
- Fat: 20g

- Carbohydrates: 12g
- Fiber: 3g
- Sugar: 4g
- Sodium: 600mg

Delight your taste buds with the essence of Mozza's culinary expertise, right in the comfort of your own home. This Wood-Grilled Swordfish with Tomato and Olive Relish is a testament to the innovative and mouthwatering creations that make Mozza a dining destination like no other.

82. Margherita Pizza with Fennel Sausage and Chili

Indulge in the exquisite flavors inspired by Nancy Silverton's Mozza restaurant with this Margherita Pizza elevated with savory fennel sausage and a hint of chili. The harmonious blend of classic Italian ingredients and bold, spicy notes creates a pizza experience that delights the senses.

Serving: 2-4 servings
Preparation time: 20 minutes
Ready time: 40 minutes

Ingredients:

For the Pizza Dough:
- 1 pound (about 450g) pizza dough, at room temperature
- All-purpose flour, for dusting

For the Toppings:
- 1 cup marinara sauce
- 8 ounces (225g) fresh mozzarella cheese, sliced
- 4 ounces (115g) fennel sausage, thinly sliced
- 1-2 red chilies, thinly sliced (adjust to taste)
- Fresh basil leaves, torn, for garnish
- Extra virgin olive oil, for drizzling

Instructions:

1. Preheat the oven to its highest temperature (usually around 500°F/260°C) and place a pizza stone or baking sheet inside to heat.
2. On a lightly floured surface, roll out the pizza dough to your desired thickness and shape.

3. Spread the marinara sauce evenly over the rolled-out dough, leaving a small border for the crust.
4. Arrange the sliced mozzarella over the sauce, followed by the fennel sausage slices and chili slices.
5. Carefully transfer the prepared pizza onto the preheated pizza stone or baking sheet.
6. Bake in the preheated oven for 12-15 minutes or until the crust is golden and the cheese has melted and slightly bubbled.
7. Once done, remove the pizza from the oven and sprinkle torn basil leaves over the hot pizza. Drizzle with a bit of extra virgin olive oil for added flavor.
8. Allow the pizza to cool for a few minutes before slicing. Serve hot and enjoy!

Nutrition Information (approximate values per serving):
Calories: 350-400 kcal
Total Fat: 15-20g
Saturated Fat: 6-8g
Cholesterol: 35-45mg
Sodium: 800-900mg
Total Carbohydrate: 35-40g
Dietary Fiber: 2-3g
Sugars: 3-5g
Protein: 15-20g
(Note: Nutritional values may vary based on specific ingredients used and portion sizes.)
This Margherita Pizza with Fennel Sausage and Chili combines the simplicity of a classic Margherita with the robust flavors of fennel sausage and a touch of heat from the chili slices. It's a delicious representation of the inventive and tantalizing dishes found at Nancy Silverton's Mozza restaurant.

83. Grilled Artichokes with Lemon Aioli

Indulge in the exquisite flavors of Mozza restaurant with these Grilled Artichokes paired perfectly with zesty Lemon Aioli. Nancy Silverton's culinary prowess shines through in this recipe, capturing the essence of the restaurant's menu and bringing it to your table. The smoky essence of grilled artichokes combined with the tangy kick of the aioli creates a delectable harmony that's sure to elevate your dining experience.

Serving: Serves 4
Preparation Time: 20 minutes
Ready Time: 45 minutes

Ingredients:
- 4 large artichokes
- 2 lemons, halved
- 4 cloves garlic, minced
- 1/4 cup olive oil
- Salt and pepper to taste

For Lemon Aioli:
- 1 cup mayonnaise
- Zest of 1 lemon
- Juice of 1 lemon
- 2 cloves garlic, minced
- 1/4 teaspoon salt
- 1/4 teaspoon black pepper
- 1 tablespoon chopped fresh parsley (optional, for garnish)

Instructions:
1. Prepare the artichokes by trimming off the top inch of the artichokes and cutting off the stem. Cut the artichokes in half lengthwise. Use a spoon to scoop out the fuzzy choke and any tough inner leaves.
2. Fill a large pot with water, squeeze in the juice of 1 lemon, and bring it to a boil. Add the prepared artichokes and cook for about 15-20 minutes or until tender when pierced with a fork. Drain and let them cool slightly.
3. In a small bowl, mix together minced garlic, juice from the remaining lemon, olive oil, salt, and pepper. Brush this mixture generously over the cooked artichokes.
4. Preheat the grill to medium-high heat. Place the artichokes on the grill, cut side down, and grill for about 5-7 minutes until lightly charred and grill marks appear. Flip and grill for an additional 3-5 minutes.
5. For the Lemon Aioli, combine mayonnaise, lemon zest, lemon juice, minced garlic, salt, and black pepper in a bowl. Mix well until thoroughly combined. Adjust seasoning to taste.
6. Serve the grilled artichokes warm with the Lemon Aioli on the side for dipping. Garnish with chopped fresh parsley if desired.

Nutrition Information:
*Note: Nutrition Information may vary based on specific ingredients used and portion sizes.
- Calories: Approximately 250 per serving
- Total Fat: 23g
- Saturated Fat: 3g
- Cholesterol: 10mg
- Sodium: 350mg
- Total Carbohydrates: 10g
- Dietary Fiber: 5g
- Sugars: 1g
- Protein: 2g

84. Wood-Roasted Mussels with Tomato and Chili

In the heart of Nancy Silverton's Mozza restaurant, the marriage of wood-fired flavors and tantalizing seafood dances in this vibrant dish. The Wood-Roasted Mussels with Tomato and Chili epitomize the culinary symphony where simplicity meets depth, creating an enticing harmony of taste and aroma.

Serving: 2-4 servings
Preparation time: 15 minutes
Ready time: 30 minutes

Ingredients:
- 2 pounds fresh mussels, cleaned and debearded
- 2 tablespoons extra-virgin olive oil
- 4 cloves garlic, finely chopped
- 1 shallot, finely chopped
- 1 red chili, thinly sliced
- 1 cup cherry tomatoes, halved
- 1/2 cup dry white wine
- 2 tablespoons chopped fresh parsley
- Salt and pepper to taste
- Crusty bread for serving

Instructions:
1. Preheat your oven to 450°F (230°C) and place a large, oven-safe pan or cast-iron skillet inside to heat.
2. In a separate pan over medium heat, add olive oil. Sauté garlic, shallot, and red chili until fragrant and slightly golden, about 2-3 minutes.
3. Add cherry tomatoes to the pan and cook for another 3-4 minutes until they start to soften.
4. Increase the heat and pour in the white wine, allowing it to simmer for 2 minutes to reduce slightly.
5. Carefully add the cleaned mussels to the hot, preheated pan or skillet in the oven. Pour the tomato and wine mixture over the mussels.
6. Roast the mussels in the oven for 6-8 minutes or until the mussels open up. Discard any that do not open.
7. Remove from the oven and sprinkle with chopped parsley. Season with salt and pepper to taste.
8. Serve immediately with crusty bread to soak up the flavorful broth.

Nutrition Information (per serving):
- Calories: 240
- Total Fat: 10g
- Saturated Fat: 1.5g
- Cholesterol: 45mg
- Sodium: 550mg
- Total Carbohydrate: 10g
- Dietary Fiber: 1g
- Sugars: 2g
- Protein: 24g
Note: Nutritional values are approximate and may vary based on specific ingredients used.

85. Shaved Brussels Sprouts and Pancetta Pizza with Balsamic

Indulge in the irresistible flavors of Nancy Silverton's Mozza restaurant with our Shaved Brussels Sprouts and Pancetta Pizza with Balsamic. This pizza creation marries the earthy essence of Brussels sprouts with the savory richness of pancetta, all drizzled with a tangy balsamic reduction.

A culinary journey awaits as you recreate the magic of Mozza in your own kitchen.

Serving: 2-4
Preparation time: 20 minutes
Ready time: 30 minutes

Ingredients:
- 1 pound pizza dough, homemade or store-bought
- 1/2 cup shredded Fontina cheese
- 1/2 cup shredded mozzarella cheese
- 1 cup Brussels sprouts, shaved
- 1/4 cup pancetta, thinly sliced
- 2 tablespoons olive oil
- Salt and pepper to taste
- 2 tablespoons balsamic reduction (store-bought or homemade)

Instructions:
1. Preheat your oven to 475°F (245°C). If you have a pizza stone, place it in the oven during the preheating.
2. In a pan over medium heat, sauté the pancetta until it becomes crispy. Remove it from the pan and set aside.
3. In the same pan, add 1 tablespoon of olive oil and sauté the shaved Brussels sprouts until they are tender but still vibrant green. Season with salt and pepper to taste. Set aside.
4. Roll out the pizza dough on a floured surface to your desired thickness.
5. If using a pizza stone, carefully transfer the rolled-out dough onto a piece of parchment paper. If not using a stone, place the dough on a lightly greased baking sheet.
6. Brush the rolled-out dough with the remaining olive oil, leaving a small border around the edges.
7. Sprinkle the shredded Fontina and mozzarella cheeses evenly over the dough.
8. Distribute the sautéed Brussels sprouts and crispy pancetta over the cheese.
9. Transfer the pizza (on parchment paper if using a stone) to the preheated oven or place the baking sheet directly in the oven.
10. Bake for 12-15 minutes or until the crust is golden and the cheese is bubbly and lightly browned.

11. Remove the pizza from the oven and drizzle with balsamic reduction.
12. Allow the pizza to cool for a few minutes before slicing and serving.

Nutrition Information:
(Per serving, based on 4 servings)
- Calories: 400
- Total Fat: 20g
- Saturated Fat: 7g
- Cholesterol: 25mg
- Sodium: 800mg
- Total Carbohydrates: 40g
- Dietary Fiber: 3g
- Sugars: 3g
- Protein: 15g
Note: Nutrition information is approximate and may vary based on specific ingredients used.

86. Burrata with Roasted Tomatoes, Pine Nuts, and Basil

Indulge in the exquisite flavors reminiscent of Nancy Silverton's Mozza restaurant with this delectable Burrata with Roasted Tomatoes, Pine Nuts, and Basil recipe. This dish captures the essence of Mozza's culinary artistry, blending creamy burrata, roasted tomatoes, toasty pine nuts, and aromatic basil. Elevate your dining experience with this harmonious combination that celebrates fresh, high-quality ingredients and the vibrant spirit of Mozza's menu.

Serving: Serves 4
Preparation Time: 15 minutes
Ready Time: 30 minutes

Ingredients:
- 4 large, ripe tomatoes, halved
- 2 tablespoons extra-virgin olive oil
- Salt and pepper, to taste
- 1/2 cup pine nuts, toasted
- 4 balls of burrata cheese

- Fresh basil leaves, for garnish
- Balsamic glaze, for drizzling (optional)

Instructions:

1. Preheat the Oven:
Preheat your oven to 375°F (190°C).
2. Roast the Tomatoes:
Place the halved tomatoes on a baking sheet, cut side up. Drizzle them with olive oil and season with salt and pepper. Roast in the preheated oven for 20-25 minutes or until the tomatoes are soft and slightly caramelized.
3. Toast the Pine Nuts:
While the tomatoes are roasting, toast the pine nuts in a dry skillet over medium heat. Stir frequently until the pine nuts are golden brown and fragrant. Remove from heat and set aside.
4. Prepare the Burrata:
Place each burrata ball on a serving plate.
5. Assemble the Dish:
Once the tomatoes are roasted, carefully place them around the burrata on the plates. Sprinkle the toasted pine nuts over the burrata and tomatoes.
6. Garnish with Basil:
Tear fresh basil leaves and scatter them over the dish for a burst of color and aromatic freshness.
7. Drizzle with Balsamic Glaze (Optional):
For an extra layer of flavor, drizzle a bit of balsamic glaze over the dish just before serving.
8. Serve and Enjoy:
Serve the Burrata with Roasted Tomatoes, Pine Nuts, and Basil immediately, allowing the creamy burrata to meld with the roasted tomatoes and aromatic basil.

Nutrition Information:

(Per serving)
- Calories: 320
- Protein: 12g
- Fat: 26g
- Carbohydrates: 10g
- Fiber: 3g
- Sugar: 6g

- Sodium: 480mg
Note: Nutrition information is approximate and may vary based on specific ingredients used. Adjust quantities accordingly for dietary preferences.

87. Grilled Shrimp and Calamari with White Beans and Lemon

Indulge your senses in the vibrant and enticing flavors inspired by the renowned menu of Nancy Silverton's Mozza restaurant with our Grilled Shrimp and Calamari with White Beans and Lemon. This exquisite dish captures the essence of Mediterranean cuisine, combining succulent seafood with wholesome white beans and the bright zest of lemon. Elevate your dining experience with this harmonious medley that embodies the culinary spirit of Mozza.

Serving: 4 servings
Preparation Time: 15 minutes
Ready Time: 30 minutes

Ingredients:
- 1 pound large shrimp, peeled and deveined
- 1 pound calamari, cleaned and cut into rings
- 2 cans (15 ounces each) white beans, drained and rinsed
- 1/4 cup extra-virgin olive oil
- 3 cloves garlic, minced
- 1 teaspoon red pepper flakes (adjust to taste)
- Salt and black pepper, to taste
- Zest of 1 lemon
- Juice of 2 lemons
- 2 tablespoons fresh parsley, chopped
- Lemon wedges for garnish

Instructions:
1. Prepare the Grill:
Preheat the grill to medium-high heat.
2. Marinate the Seafood:

In a large bowl, combine the shrimp and calamari. Drizzle with olive oil, add minced garlic, red pepper flakes, salt, and black pepper. Toss to coat the seafood evenly in the marinade. Let it marinate for 10 minutes.
3. Grill the Seafood:
Thread the marinated shrimp and calamari onto skewers. Grill for 2-3 minutes per side or until the seafood is cooked through and has a beautiful char.
4. Warm the White Beans:
In a saucepan over medium heat, warm the white beans. Add lemon zest, lemon juice, and a drizzle of olive oil. Season with salt and black pepper to taste. Stir in chopped parsley.
5. Assemble the Dish:
Arrange a generous portion of warm white beans on each plate. Top with the grilled shrimp and calamari skewers.
6. Garnish and Serve:
Garnish the dish with additional chopped parsley and lemon wedges. Serve immediately, allowing the vibrant flavors to shine.

Nutrition Information:
(Per Serving)
- Calories: 450
- Protein: 30g
- Carbohydrates: 35g
- Fat: 20g
- Fiber: 8g

Indulge in this tantalizing seafood creation that mirrors the culinary excellence found at Nancy Silverton's Mozza restaurant. With its harmonious blend of grilled shrimp, calamari, and white beans, each bite is a celebration of Mediterranean flavors that will leave your taste buds craving more.

88. Wood-Grilled Ribeye with Truffle Butter and Parmesan

Indulge your senses in the culinary excellence inspired by Nancy Silverton's Mozza restaurant with this tantalizing recipe for Wood-Grilled Ribeye with Truffle Butter and Parmesan. Elevating the art of grilling, this dish captures the essence of Mozza's dedication to quality ingredients and exquisite flavors. The combination of a perfectly wood-grilled ribeye, decadent truffle butter, and rich Parmesan creates a symphony of taste that will leave your palate craving for more. It's a celebration of prime ingredients and culinary craftsmanship, inviting you to experience the magic of Mozza in your own kitchen.

Serving: 4 servings
Preparation Time: 15 minutes
Ready Time: 35 minutes

Ingredients:
- 4 bone-in ribeye steaks (1.5 inches thick)
- Salt and black pepper, to taste
- 4 tablespoons truffle butter
- 1/2 cup freshly grated Parmesan cheese
- 2 tablespoons olive oil
- 1 tablespoon fresh thyme leaves, for garnish

Instructions:
1. Preheat your wood grill to medium-high heat. Season the ribeye steaks generously with salt and black pepper.
2. Place the seasoned ribeye steaks on the preheated grill and cook for approximately 8-10 minutes per side, or until they reach your desired level of doneness. For a medium-rare steak, aim for an internal temperature of 130°F (54°C).
3. During the last few minutes of grilling, place a tablespoon of truffle butter on top of each steak, allowing it to melt and infuse the meat with its luxurious flavor.
4. Once the ribeye steaks are cooked to perfection, remove them from the grill and let them rest for 5 minutes to allow the juices to redistribute.
5. Drizzle olive oil over the steaks and sprinkle freshly grated Parmesan cheese on top. The heat from the steak will melt the cheese slightly.
6. Garnish with fresh thyme leaves for a fragrant and herbal touch.
7. Serve the Wood-Grilled Ribeye with Truffle Butter and Parmesan alongside your favorite sides or a simple arugula salad to complement the richness of the dish.

Nutrition Information:
(Per serving)
- Calories: 650

- Protein: 48g
- Fat: 49g
- Carbohydrates: 1g
- Fiber: 0g
- Sugar: 0g
- Sodium: 780mg

Note: Nutrition information is approximate and may vary based on specific ingredients used.

89. Prosciutto and Burrata Bruschetta with Fig Jam

Indulge your taste buds in a symphony of flavors with this exquisite Prosciutto and Burrata Bruschetta with Fig Jam, inspired by the culinary wonders of Nancy Silverton's renowned Mozza restaurant. This delightful bruschetta combines the richness of burrata cheese, the saltiness of prosciutto, and the sweet elegance of fig jam, creating a harmonious blend that is sure to elevate your dining experience. Perfect for entertaining or savoring a moment of culinary bliss, this dish captures the essence of Mozza's sophisticated yet approachable menu.

Serving: Makes 4 servings.
Preparation Time: 15 minutes.
Ready Time: 15 minutes.

Ingredients:
- 1 baguette, sliced into ½-inch thick pieces
- 8 ounces burrata cheese, at room temperature
- 8 slices prosciutto
- 1/2 cup fig jam
- Freshly ground black pepper, to taste
- Fresh basil leaves, for garnish

Instructions:
1. Preheat the Oven: Preheat your oven to 375°F (190°C).
2. Toast the Baguette: Place the baguette slices on a baking sheet and toast them in the preheated oven for about 5 minutes or until golden brown.

3. Assemble the Bruschetta: Spread a generous spoonful of burrata on each toasted baguette slice. Top with a slice of prosciutto, allowing it to drape over the burrata.
4. Add Fig Jam: Spoon a dollop of fig jam onto each bruschetta. Drizzle with a touch of honey for extra sweetness, if desired.
5. Season and Garnish: Sprinkle freshly ground black pepper over the bruschetta to taste. Garnish with fresh basil leaves for a burst of color and aromatic freshness.
6. Serve: Arrange the bruschetta on a serving platter and serve immediately.

Nutrition Information:
(Per Serving)
- Calories: 320
- Total Fat: 12g
- Saturated Fat: 6g
- Trans Fat: 0g
- Cholesterol: 30mg
- Sodium: 580mg
- Total Carbohydrates: 42g
- Dietary Fiber: 2g
- Sugars: 16g
- Protein: 12g

Savor the sophistication of Mozza's culinary artistry with every bite of this Prosciutto and Burrata Bruschetta with Fig Jam, a tantalizing blend of textures and flavors that will leave your palate longing for more.

90. Margherita Pizza with Eggplant and Ricotta

Indulge your taste buds in a culinary journey inspired by the renowned Nancy Silverton's Mozza restaurant with our twist on the classic Margherita Pizza. Elevate the traditional flavors by adding roasted eggplant and creamy ricotta, creating a delightful fusion that is both sophisticated and comforting. This recipe promises a symphony of textures and tastes that will transport you to the heart of Mozza's exceptional culinary experience.

Serving: 4 servings

Preparation Time: 20 minutes
Ready Time: 30 minutes

Ingredients:

- 1 pound pizza dough, at room temperature
- 1 cup marinara sauce
- 1 large eggplant, thinly sliced
- 1 cup ricotta cheese
- 1 1/2 cups fresh mozzarella, sliced
- 1/4 cup fresh basil leaves, torn
- 2 tablespoons extra-virgin olive oil
- Salt and black pepper to taste
- Cornmeal or flour for dusting

Instructions:

1. Preheat the Oven:
Preheat your oven to 475°F (245°C). If you have a pizza stone, place it in the oven to heat.
2. Prepare the Eggplant:
Lay out the eggplant slices on a baking sheet. Drizzle with olive oil, season with salt and pepper, and roast in the preheated oven for about 10 minutes, or until the slices are tender and slightly golden.
3. Roll Out the Dough:
Dust your work surface with flour or cornmeal. Roll out the pizza dough to your desired thickness. If you have a pizza peel, transfer the rolled-out dough onto it.
4. Assemble the Pizza:
Spread the marinara sauce evenly over the rolled-out dough, leaving a small border for the crust. Arrange the roasted eggplant slices on top. Dot the pizza with spoonfuls of ricotta and distribute the fresh mozzarella slices evenly.
5. Bake the Pizza:
If using a pizza stone, carefully transfer the pizza onto the hot stone in the oven. Bake for 12-15 minutes or until the crust is golden and the cheese is bubbly and slightly browned.
6. Finish and Serve:
Once out of the oven, sprinkle torn fresh basil leaves over the hot pizza. Drizzle with a bit of extra-virgin olive oil. Allow the pizza to cool for a few minutes before slicing.

Nutrition Information:
Per Serving:
- Calories: 450
- Total Fat: 20g
- Saturated Fat: 8g
- Cholesterol: 35mg
- Sodium: 900mg
- Total Carbohydrates: 50g
- Dietary Fiber: 5g
- Sugars: 6g
- Protein: 15g

Elevate your pizza night with this Margherita Pizza featuring the unique flavors of eggplant and ricotta—a true homage to the culinary excellence of Nancy Silverton's Mozza restaurant. Enjoy!

91. Wood-Grilled Pork Chops with Apple and Mustard

Indulge in the tantalizing flavors reminiscent of the renowned Mozza restaurant, inspired by Nancy Silverton's culinary finesse. These wood-grilled pork chops with apple and mustard showcase the perfect harmony of smoky, savory, and subtly sweet notes, creating a culinary masterpiece that's both comforting and sophisticated.

Serving: 4 servings
Preparation time: 15 minutes
Ready time: 30 minutes

Ingredients:
- 4 bone-in pork chops (about 1 inch thick)
- 2 tablespoons olive oil
- Salt and freshly ground black pepper, to taste
- 2 apples, cored and thinly sliced
- 2 tablespoons whole grain mustard
- 2 tablespoons honey
- 2 cloves garlic, minced
- 1 teaspoon fresh thyme leaves
- Wood chips (preferably applewood), soaked in water for 30 minutes

Instructions:
1. Preheat the grill to medium-high heat and prepare it for indirect grilling. Place soaked wood chips directly on the coals or in a smoker box for a gas grill.
2. Pat dry the pork chops with paper towels. Brush them lightly with olive oil and season generously with salt and pepper.
3. In a bowl, combine the sliced apples, whole grain mustard, honey, minced garlic, and fresh thyme. Toss until the apples are evenly coated.
4. Grill the pork chops over indirect heat, covered, for about 4-5 minutes per side or until they reach an internal temperature of 145°F (63°C). During the last few minutes of grilling, place the apple mixture on the grill in a heatproof dish to warm through.
5. Once done, transfer the pork chops to a plate and let them rest for 5 minutes, tented with foil.
6. Serve the wood-grilled pork chops topped with the warm apple and mustard mixture.

Nutrition Information: *(per serving)*
- Calories: 380
- Total Fat: 18g
- Saturated Fat: 5g
- Cholesterol: 105mg
- Sodium: 210mg
- Total Carbohydrate: 17g
- Dietary Fiber: 2g
- Sugars: 13g
- Protein: 36g

Enjoy this delectable dish that captures the essence of Mozza's culinary prowess, delivering a blend of rustic flavors that will delight your taste buds and elevate your dining experience.

92. Roasted Beet and Goat Cheese Pizza with Arugula

This Roasted Beet and Goat Cheese Pizza with Arugula is a tribute to the vibrant flavors found at Nancy Silverton's iconic Mozza restaurant. It combines earthy roasted beets, creamy goat cheese, and peppery arugula atop a crispy pizza crust for a delightful culinary experience that balances richness and freshness in every bite.

Serving: Serves: 4
Preparation time: 20 minutes
Ready time: 40 minutes
Nutrition information: (per serving)
- Calories: XXX
- Carbohydrates: XXX
- Protein: XXX
- Fat: XXX
- Fiber: XXX

Ingredients:
- 1 pound pizza dough
- 3 medium beets, roasted and sliced
- 4 ounces goat cheese, crumbled
- 2 cups arugula
- Olive oil
- Salt and pepper, to taste
- Balsamic glaze (optional)

Instructions:
1. Preheat and Prep: Preheat your oven to 450°F (230°C). If the beets aren't roasted yet, wrap them in foil and roast in the oven for about 40-50 minutes until tender. Let them cool, then peel and slice into rounds.
2. Prepare Pizza Dough: Roll out the pizza dough on a floured surface into your desired shape. Place it on a baking sheet or a pizza stone.
3. Assemble the Pizza: Drizzle olive oil over the dough. Arrange the roasted beet slices evenly on top. Sprinkle crumbled goat cheese over the beets. Season with salt and pepper to taste.
4. Bake: Place the pizza in the preheated oven and bake for 15-20 minutes, or until the crust is golden brown and the cheese is bubbly.
5. Finish and Serve: Once out of the oven, scatter fresh arugula over the hot pizza. Drizzle a bit of olive oil and balsamic glaze if desired. Slice and serve immediately.

Nutrition Information:
Nutritional values may vary based on specific ingredients used. Here's an approximate breakdown per serving:

- Calories: XXX
- Carbohydrates: XXX grams
- Protein: XXX grams
- Fat: XXX grams
- Fiber: XXX grams

Enjoy this Roasted Beet and Goat Cheese Pizza with Arugula as a delightful representation of the incredible flavors found at Nancy Silverton's Mozza restaurant!

93. Burrata with Prosciutto, Figs, and Balsamic

Indulge in the exquisite flavors of Nancy Silverton's Mozza restaurant with this delightful dish. Creamy burrata, savory prosciutto, sweet figs, and tangy balsamic combine for a taste sensation that embodies the restaurant's renowned culinary expertise.

Serving: 4 servings
Preparation time: 15 minutes
Ready time: 15 minutes

Ingredients:
- 4 balls of burrata cheese
- 8 slices of prosciutto
- 8 fresh figs, quartered
- 4 tablespoons balsamic glaze
- Freshly ground black pepper
- Fresh basil leaves for garnish

Instructions:
1. Prepare the Ingredients: Take the burrata out of the refrigerator to come to room temperature for about 15-20 minutes. Meanwhile, quarter the fresh figs and set aside. Arrange the prosciutto slices on a serving platter.
2. Assemble the Dish: Place each burrata ball onto the serving platter, on top of the prosciutto slices. Surround the burrata with the quartered figs, distributing them evenly.

3. Drizzle with Balsamic: Drizzle each burrata ball and the figs with balsamic glaze. Add a twist of freshly ground black pepper for a touch of spice.
4. Garnish and Serve: Garnish the dish with fresh basil leaves for added freshness and aroma.
5. Serve: Serve immediately to enjoy the contrast of creamy, savory, sweet, and tangy flavors.

Nutrition Information (per serving):
- Calories: 320
- Total Fat: 22g
- Saturated Fat: 12g
- Cholesterol: 65mg
- Sodium: 900mg
- Total Carbohydrates: 17g
- Dietary Fiber: 4g
- Sugars: 10g
- Protein: 16g

Note: Nutrition Information may vary based on specific brands used for ingredients.
This dish encapsulates the simplicity and elegance found at Nancy Silverton's Mozza, offering a burst of flavors that harmonize beautifully on the palate.

94. Grilled Radicchio with Gorgonzola and Walnuts

Discover the bold and sophisticated flavors inspired by the renowned menu of Nancy Silverton's Mozza restaurant with this delectable recipe for Grilled Radicchio with Gorgonzola and Walnuts. This dish embodies the perfect balance of smoky, bitter radicchio, creamy Gorgonzola, and crunchy walnuts—a true celebration of textures and tastes. It's a delightful addition to any table, showcasing the culinary finesse that defines the Mozza experience.

Serving: 4 servings
Preparation Time: 15 minutes
Ready Time: 25 minutes

Ingredients:

- 2 large heads of radicchio, quartered
- 1/4 cup extra-virgin olive oil
- Salt and black pepper, to taste
- 1 cup Gorgonzola cheese, crumbled
- 1/2 cup walnuts, toasted and coarsely chopped

Instructions:

1. Preheat the grill to medium-high heat.
2. In a large bowl, drizzle the radicchio quarters with olive oil, ensuring they are evenly coated. Season with salt and black pepper to taste.
3. Place the radicchio quarters on the preheated grill. Grill for 3-4 minutes per side, or until the leaves are slightly charred and wilted. The goal is to achieve a balance of smokiness and tenderness.
4. Remove the grilled radicchio from the heat and arrange the quarters on a serving platter.
5. While the radicchio is still warm, sprinkle the crumbled Gorgonzola evenly over the top, allowing it to melt slightly.
6. Finish the dish by scattering the toasted and chopped walnuts over the radicchio and Gorgonzola.
7. Serve immediately, allowing the cheese to melt further and the flavors to meld together.

Nutrition Information:

(Per serving)

- Calories: 320
- Fat: 28g
- Saturated Fat: 7g
- Cholesterol: 20mg
- Sodium: 480mg
- Carbohydrates: 9g
- Fiber: 4g
- Sugar: 3g
- Protein: 10g

Elevate your culinary experience with the exquisite combination of grilled radicchio, Gorgonzola, and walnuts—a dish that captures the essence of Nancy Silverton's Mozza restaurant in every bite.

95. Wood-Roasted Chicken with Lemon and Thyme

Indulge in the rustic charm of Nancy Silverton's Mozza restaurant with our Wood-Roasted Chicken with Lemon and Thyme recipe. Inspired by the culinary finesse of Mozza, this dish captures the essence of bold flavors and impeccable simplicity. The wood-roasting technique imparts a smoky depth, while the zesty notes of lemon and the earthy aroma of thyme elevate the chicken to culinary perfection. Gather around the table and savor the essence of Mozza in the comfort of your own home.

Serving: 4 servings
Preparation Time: 15 minutes
Ready Time: 1 hour and 30 minutes

Ingredients:
- 1 whole chicken (approximately 4 pounds)
- 2 lemons, sliced
- 4 cloves garlic, minced
- 2 tablespoons fresh thyme leaves
- 2 tablespoons olive oil
- Salt and black pepper to taste

Instructions:
1. Preheat the Oven:
- Preheat your oven to 400°F (200°C).
2. Prepare the Chicken:
- Rinse the chicken under cold water and pat it dry with paper towels.
- Season the chicken generously with salt and black pepper, both inside and out.
3. Stuff and Truss:
- Stuff the cavity of the chicken with sliced lemons, minced garlic, and fresh thyme leaves.
- Truss the chicken using kitchen twine to ensure even cooking.
4. Rub with Olive Oil:
- Drizzle the olive oil over the chicken, spreading it evenly to coat the skin.
5. Wood-Roasting:
- Place the seasoned and trussed chicken on a roasting pan.
- Roast the chicken in the preheated oven for approximately 1 hour and 15 minutes or until the internal temperature reaches 165°F (74°C).

- Baste the chicken with its juices halfway through the cooking time.
6. Rest and Serve:
- Allow the chicken to rest for 10 minutes before carving.
- Serve the wood-roasted chicken with lemon and thyme on a platter, garnished with additional fresh thyme leaves and lemon slices.

Nutrition Information:
Note: Nutrition information is approximate and may vary based on specific ingredients used.
- Calories per serving: 350
- Protein: 25g
- Carbohydrates: 2g
- Fat: 27g
- Saturated Fat: 7g
- Cholesterol: 120mg
- Sodium: 600mg
- Fiber: 1g
- Sugar: 0g

Savor the rich flavors of Mozza's wood-roasted chicken with lemon and thyme, a dish that embodies the culinary spirit of Nancy Silverton's renowned restaurant.

96. Margherita Pizza with Roasted Garlic and Ricotta

Indulge in the culinary magic inspired by the renowned Nancy Silverton's Mozza restaurant with our twist on the classic Margherita Pizza. Elevate your pizza experience with the rich flavors of roasted garlic and creamy ricotta, making each bite a symphony of taste. This recipe captures the essence of Mozza's dedication to fresh, high-quality ingredients and inventive combinations that define the restaurant's distinctive menu.

Serving: Makes 1 large pizza (8 slices)
Preparation Time: 20 minutes
Ready Time: 30 minutes

Ingredients:
- 1 pound pizza dough, at room temperature

- 1/4 cup extra-virgin olive oil
- 3 cloves garlic, minced
- 1 1/2 cups fresh mozzarella, sliced
- 1 cup cherry tomatoes, halved
- 1/4 cup fresh basil leaves, torn
- Salt and black pepper to taste
- 1/2 cup ricotta cheese

Instructions:

1. Preheat your oven to 475°F (245°C).
2. In a small skillet, heat the olive oil over medium heat. Add the minced garlic and sauté until fragrant, about 1-2 minutes. Remove from heat and set aside.
3. Roll out the pizza dough on a floured surface to your desired thickness.
4. Transfer the rolled-out dough to a pizza stone or baking sheet.
5. Brush the dough with the garlic-infused olive oil, leaving a small border around the edges.
6. Evenly distribute the fresh mozzarella slices and cherry tomato halves over the dough. Season with salt and black pepper to taste.
7. Bake in the preheated oven for 12-15 minutes or until the crust is golden and the cheese is melted and bubbly.
8. Remove the pizza from the oven and let it cool for a couple of minutes.
9. Dollop spoonfuls of ricotta cheese over the hot pizza.
10. Scatter torn basil leaves over the top, and slice the pizza into 8 pieces.

Nutrition Information:

Note: Nutritional values are approximate and may vary based on specific ingredients used and portion sizes.

- Calories: 280 per slice
- Total Fat: 12g
- Saturated Fat: 5g
- Trans Fat: 0g
- Cholesterol: 20mg
- Sodium: 480mg
- Total Carbohydrates: 30g
- Dietary Fiber: 2g
- Sugars: 2g
- Protein: 12g

Elevate your pizza night with this Margherita Pizza featuring roasted garlic and ricotta—a taste sensation straight from the inspiration of Nancy Silverton's Mozza restaurant. Enjoy!

97. Ricotta and Swiss Chard Ravioli with Brown Butter and Sage

Indulge in the rich flavors of Mozza-inspired cuisine with these exquisite Ricotta and Swiss Chard Ravioli with Brown Butter and Sage. This dish pays homage to the culinary finesse of Nancy Silverton's renowned Mozza restaurant, where every bite is a celebration of quality ingredients and expert craftsmanship. Elevate your dining experience with this delightful blend of fresh ricotta, vibrant Swiss chard, and the nutty warmth of brown butter and sage.

Serving: 4 servings
Preparation Time: 30 minutes
Ready Time: 1 hour

Ingredients:
- 2 cups fresh ricotta cheese
- 1 cup cooked and finely chopped Swiss chard
- 1/2 cup grated Parmesan cheese
- 1 egg
- Salt and pepper to taste
- 1 package of wonton or pasta wrappers
- 1/2 cup unsalted butter
- Fresh sage leaves for garnish
- Additional Parmesan for serving

Instructions:
1. Prepare the Filling:
- In a bowl, combine the fresh ricotta, cooked Swiss chard, grated Parmesan, and the egg.
- Season with salt and pepper to taste.
- Mix the ingredients thoroughly until well combined.
2. Assemble the Ravioli:
- Lay out the wonton or pasta wrappers on a clean surface.

- Place a spoonful of the ricotta and Swiss chard filling in the center of each wrapper.
- Moisten the edges of the wrapper with water and fold it over, sealing the edges to form a ravioli shape.
- Repeat until all the filling is used.
3. Cook the Ravioli:
- Bring a large pot of salted water to a gentle boil.
- Carefully drop the ravioli into the boiling water and cook until they float to the surface, indicating they are done (usually 2-3 minutes).
- Remove the ravioli with a slotted spoon and set aside.
4. Prepare the Brown Butter and Sage Sauce:
- In a skillet, melt the unsalted butter over medium heat.
- Add fresh sage leaves to the melted butter and cook until the butter turns a golden brown color and the sage leaves become crispy.
5. Serve:
- Plate the cooked ravioli and drizzle the brown butter and sage sauce over the top.
- Garnish with additional Parmesan cheese.
- Serve immediately and savor the exquisite flavors.

Nutrition Information:
(Per serving)
- Calories: 450 kcal
- Protein: 18g
- Carbohydrates: 28g
- Fat: 30g
- Fiber: 2g

Elevate your dining experience with the inspired combination of fresh ingredients and the culinary expertise that defines the menu at Nancy Silverton's Mozza restaurant.

98. Wood-Grilled Halibut with Lemon and Herb Pesto

Indulge your senses with the tantalizing flavors of Nancy Silverton's Mozza restaurant right in your own home. This recipe captures the essence of Mozza's culinary mastery with its Wood-Grilled Halibut adorned with a zesty Lemon and Herb Pesto. The combination of smoky, grilled halibut and the vibrant freshness of the pesto creates a dish that is not only visually stunning but also a celebration of exquisite taste. Elevate your dining experience with this homage to the culinary genius of Nancy Silverton.

Serving: 4 servings
Preparation Time: 20 minutes
Ready Time: 30 minutes

Ingredients:
- 4 halibut fillets (about 6 ounces each)
- 2 tablespoons olive oil
- Salt and black pepper, to taste

For the Lemon and Herb Pesto:
- 1 cup fresh basil leaves
- 1/2 cup fresh parsley leaves
- 1/4 cup pine nuts, toasted
- 2 cloves garlic, peeled
- 1/2 cup grated Parmesan cheese
- Zest of 1 lemon
- Juice of 1 lemon
- 1/2 cup extra-virgin olive oil
- Salt and black pepper, to taste

Instructions:
1. Prepare the Halibut:
- Preheat the grill to medium-high heat.
- Brush the halibut fillets with olive oil and season with salt and black pepper.
2. Grill the Halibut:
- Place the halibut fillets on the preheated grill.
- Grill for about 4-5 minutes per side or until the fish is cooked through and has a delightful smoky flavor.
- Remove the halibut from the grill and set aside.
3. Make the Lemon and Herb Pesto:
- In a food processor, combine basil, parsley, pine nuts, garlic, Parmesan cheese, lemon zest, and lemon juice.
- Pulse until the ingredients are finely chopped.
- With the processor running, slowly drizzle in the olive oil until the pesto reaches a smooth consistency.

- Season with salt and black pepper to taste.
4. Serve:
- Place grilled halibut fillets on serving plates.
- Spoon a generous amount of Lemon and Herb Pesto over each fillet.
- Garnish with additional lemon zest and fresh herbs if desired.

Nutrition Information:
- *(Note: Nutritional values are approximate and may vary based on specific ingredients and portion sizes.)*
- Calories per serving: XXX
- Protein: XXX g
- Carbohydrates: XXX g
- Fat: XXX g
- Fiber: XXX g
- Sugar: XXX g
- Sodium: XXX mg

Enjoy the symphony of flavors in every bite of this Wood-Grilled Halibut with Lemon and Herb Pesto—a dish inspired by the culinary wonders of Nancy Silverton's Mozza restaurant!

99. Panzanella Salad with Grilled Vegetables and Feta

Indulge in the vibrant flavors of Nancy Silverton's Mozza restaurant with this delightful Panzanella Salad featuring Grilled Vegetables and Feta. A celebration of fresh, seasonal produce combined with the bold Mediterranean-inspired twist, this salad captures the essence of Mozza's innovative menu. Perfect for a light lunch or a refreshing side dish, this Panzanella Salad is a symphony of textures and tastes that will transport your taste buds straight to the heart of culinary excellence.

Serving: 4 servings
Preparation Time: 15 minutes
Ready Time: 30 minutes

Ingredients:
- 4 cups day-old rustic bread, cut into bite-sized cubes
- 2 cups cherry tomatoes, halved

- 1 large cucumber, sliced
- 1 red bell pepper, sliced
- 1 yellow bell pepper, sliced
- 1 red onion, thinly sliced
- 1/4 cup Kalamata olives, pitted and halved
- 1/2 cup crumbled feta cheese
- 1/4 cup fresh basil leaves, torn

For the Grilled Vegetables:
- 2 tablespoons olive oil
- 1 teaspoon balsamic vinegar
- 1 teaspoon dried oregano
- Salt and pepper to taste

For the Dressing:
- 1/4 cup extra-virgin olive oil
- 2 tablespoons red wine vinegar
- 1 teaspoon Dijon mustard
- 1 garlic clove, minced
- Salt and pepper to taste

Instructions:

1. Grill the Vegetables:
- Preheat the grill to medium-high heat.
- In a bowl, whisk together olive oil, balsamic vinegar, dried oregano, salt, and pepper.
- Toss the sliced bell peppers and red onion in the marinade.
- Grill the vegetables until they are charred and tender, about 5-7 minutes. Set aside.

2. Prepare the Dressing:
- In a small bowl, whisk together the extra-virgin olive oil, red wine vinegar, Dijon mustard, minced garlic, salt, and pepper. Set aside.

3. Assemble the Salad:
- In a large bowl, combine the bread cubes, cherry tomatoes, cucumber, grilled vegetables, Kalamata olives, and torn basil leaves.
- Drizzle the dressing over the salad and toss gently to combine, ensuring the bread cubes soak up the flavors.

4. Add the Finishing Touch:
- Sprinkle the crumbled feta cheese over the top of the salad, adding a creamy and tangy element to the mix.

5. Serve:
- Allow the salad to rest for a few minutes to let the flavors meld.

- Serve in individual bowls or on a platter, garnished with extra basil leaves if desired.

Nutrition Information:
(Per serving)
- Calories: 350
- Protein: 8g
- Carbohydrates: 40g
- Fiber: 6g
- Sugar: 8g
- Fat: 18g
- Saturated Fat: 4g
- Cholesterol: 15mg
- Sodium: 600mg

Enjoy this Panzanella Salad with Grilled Vegetables and Feta as a testament to the culinary brilliance that defines Nancy Silverton's Mozza restaurant.

100. Burrata with Roasted Red Peppers, Pesto, and Pine Nuts

Indulge your senses in the exquisite flavors inspired by the renowned menu of Nancy Silverton's Mozza restaurant with our Burrata with Roasted Red Peppers, Pesto, and Pine Nuts recipe. This dish captures the essence of Mozza's culinary artistry, combining creamy burrata, smoky roasted red peppers, vibrant pesto, and the nutty crunch of pine nuts. Elevate your dining experience with this delectable dish that effortlessly balances richness and freshness.

Serving: 4 servings
Preparation Time: 15 minutes
Ready Time: 25 minutes

Ingredients:
- 4 large balls of fresh burrata
- 2 red bell peppers, roasted, peeled, and sliced
- 1/2 cup pine nuts, toasted
- Fresh basil leaves for garnish

For the Pesto:
- 2 cups fresh basil leaves, packed
- 1/2 cup grated Parmesan cheese
- 1/2 cup extra-virgin olive oil
- 1/4 cup pine nuts, toasted
- 2 cloves garlic, peeled
- Salt and pepper to taste

Instructions:

1. Prepare the Pesto:
- In a food processor, combine the basil, Parmesan, pine nuts, and garlic.
- Pulse until coarsely chopped.
- With the processor running, slowly pour in the olive oil until the pesto reaches a smooth consistency.
- Season with salt and pepper to taste. Set aside.

2. Roast Red Peppers:
- Preheat the oven broiler.
- Place the red peppers on a baking sheet and broil, turning occasionally, until the skin is charred and blistered.
- Transfer the peppers to a bowl, cover with plastic wrap, and let them steam for 10 minutes.
- Peel off the skins, remove seeds, and slice the peppers into strips.

3. Assemble the Burrata Dish:
- Arrange the burrata on a serving platter.
- Spoon the roasted red pepper strips over and around the burrata.
- Drizzle the pesto generously over the burrata and peppers.
- Sprinkle toasted pine nuts on top for a delightful crunch.
- Garnish with fresh basil leaves.

4. Serve:
- Serve immediately, allowing the burrata to be the star with its creamy center complemented by the vibrant flavors of pesto and roasted red peppers.

Nutrition Information:
- *Note: Nutritional values are approximate.*
- Calories per serving: XXX
- Fat: XXg
- Saturated Fat: XXg
- Cholesterol: XXmg
- Sodium: XXXmg

- Carbohydrates: XXg
- Fiber: XXg
- Sugar: XXg
- Protein: XXg

Enjoy this Mozza-inspired Burrata creation, a symphony of textures and flavors that will transport you to the heart of culinary excellence!

CONCLUSION

In the delightful journey through the pages of "Mozza Magic: A Culinary Journey with 100 Inspired Creations from Nancy Silverton's Iconic Restaurant," the essence of culinary artistry unfolds, bringing to life the unique and vibrant flavors that define the renowned Mozza restaurant. As we conclude this culinary adventure, it becomes evident that the cookbook is not merely a collection of recipes; rather, it is a celebration of creativity, passion, and the indelible mark left by Nancy Silverton on the world of gastronomy.

One cannot help but marvel at the diverse array of dishes presented in the cookbook, each a testament to the culinary genius that is Nancy Silverton. The 100 inspired creations that grace the pages are a harmonious blend of tradition and innovation, showcasing the chef's commitment to pushing culinary boundaries while paying homage to the rich culinary heritage that informs Mozza's menu.

One of the defining features of "Mozza Magic" is its ability to demystify the seemingly complex dishes associated with fine dining. Silverton's approachable and informative narrative style transforms each recipe into a culinary lesson, inviting both seasoned chefs and novice home cooks alike to embark on a culinary journey that transcends the boundaries of the kitchen.

The cookbook not only provides detailed instructions on recreating Mozza's iconic dishes but also encourages readers to infuse their creations with a personal touch. It is a tribute to the creative spirit that lies within every cook, urging them to experiment, adapt, and make each dish uniquely their own. Through this, the cookbook becomes a catalyst for culinary exploration, inspiring readers to go beyond the confines of a recipe and embrace the joy of culinary improvisation.

As we navigate through the pages, it becomes clear that "Mozza Magic" is more than just a compilation of recipes – it is a glimpse into the philosophy that defines Nancy Silverton's approach to food. The emphasis on quality ingredients, meticulous attention to detail, and a deep respect for the culinary traditions that form the foundation of each dish are threads woven throughout the cookbook. In essence, it is a guide not just to cooking but to understanding and appreciating the artistry that goes into creating a memorable dining experience.

Beyond the kitchen, "Mozza Magic" also serves as a tribute to the communal aspect of food. Silverton's recipes are an invitation to gather around the table, share stories, and savor the joys of good company. The cookbook becomes a medium through which the spirit of Mozza transcends the restaurant walls and finds a place in the homes and hearts of those who embark on this culinary journey.

In conclusion, "Mozza Magic: A Culinary Journey with 100 Inspired Creations from Nancy Silverton's Iconic Restaurant" is more than a cookbook – it is a culinary odyssey that invites readers to explore the intersection of tradition and innovation, indulge in the pleasures of experimentation, and savor the magic that happens when passion and creativity come together in the kitchen. As we close the pages, the lingering aroma of Mozza's inspired creations lingers, leaving an indelible mark on the palates and imaginations of all who embark on this gastronomic adventure.

Printed in Poland
by Amazon Fulfillment
Poland Sp. z o.o., Wrocław

54274570R00096